BE MORE LIKE YOU

A Guide to Answering the Ultimate Question "What do I want to do with my life?"

Tyler Lafferty

This book is dedicated to my family –
Kelly, Allie, Lauren and Ryan

Your inspiration is scattered throughout these pages.
To you, I am forever grateful.

Contents

Preface

I hold a deep-rooted belief that we have an obligation to ourselves to align our unique skills and interests to an industry and profession that we're passionate about. In doing so, we honor our real, authentic being and in this place we find true fulfillment and happiness. Said a little more simply and with a lot more gusto:

Do what you love!
Carpe Diem!
You only live once (YOLO)!
Follow your dreams!
Be More Like You!

There is an innate curiosity and interest inside of each of us, cultivated by our experiences, that reflects our true self. Our true being. Why does this grab my attention, but that doesn't? Why do I enjoy lacrosse over bowling? Why is geology more interesting to me than astronomy? Why do I love after school theater club, but not horseback riding? This is the intersection between you and all of the things that have influenced your life.

When these interests are cultivated and we spend more time living into them, ultimately they turn into our passions. Canadian psychology researcher Robert Vallerand concluded "passion is what makes life worth living."

He acknowledges two types of passion: obsessive and harmonious. People with obsessive passion sometimes feel negative pressure to participate in the activities they view as important and believe that the outcome of those activities define them. Think of the volleyball player who feels like she *has* to practice, practice, practice and then has a bad game and sees herself as a loser.

On the other hand, Vallerand says people with harmonious passion feel a sense of freedom and fulfillment while participating in their interests and understand the outcomes of those pursuits don't necessarily define them; they're just happy doing them. Think of a moment you were doing something and completely lost track of time because you were having so much fun.

Our passions, when understood and cultivated in a healthy manner, can be a true source of enjoyment. Life is too short not to do whatever we can to truly align with these traits when deciding how to spend our time, especially with our professional aspirations. On average, our careers consume 45 years of our lives. Imagine, 45 years! That's a long time doing something you're not passionate about or rather "just paying the bills."

For more than 20 years, I've been captivated with finding ways of helping young people identify and build career paths they're passionate about. This started with being a guest speaker at educational conferences and in classrooms. Offering countless informational interviews, job shadows and internships. Mentoring high school and college students. Sitting on educational advisory boards. Funding experimental schools. Building an online software platform connecting industry professionals with educators in order to raise awareness with students about different career paths. And ultimately writing this book.

My story is fairly simple and mirrors both the main character, Rory, and then his mentor, C.J. Like Rory, I found myself in college and questioning my path. Did I really want to be in the FBI? If not, getting this political science degree and then law degree seemed like a fairly useless track. Aside from hearing a few stories from my friend's Dad, who was in the FBI, and watching a few crime dramas on television, I really didn't know much about the day-to-day job. Before that, I had talked about being a dentist. I couldn't even tell you the genesis of that idea. If I'm honest with myself, I think both sounded like good professions that seem to satisfy people when the barrage of questions around graduation started. "What do you want to do with your life? What are you going to study in college? Do you actually have a plan?"

These questions can seem daunting if you don't have a good answer; and even if you do, devising a plan to get there can feel intimidating. I think oftentimes we cling to a fleeting idea and then it becomes reality, whether we meant it to or not. You have to start signing up for classes and setting a direction. I appreciated that my high school tried to have us take vocational tests to determine what we want to do someday. No joke, I think mine said a forest ranger or sanitation specialist (garbage man). They may have been over indexing on my answer to, "Do you enjoy being outside?"

I take full responsibility for finding myself in that position of doubting my political science/law school/FBI career path. I hadn't really taken much time at all to seriously consider what I was interested in. Or what I was good at. And I certainly wasn't thinking about what industry, if I chose it for my career, would truly bring me joy. I just needed to pick a major, get a degree and get a job. That's what you did to be successful. Whether you really enjoyed it or not, well, that was a bonus.

So there I sat, early in my junior year of college, already pretty far down the path of a political science degree with no direct correlation to a professional objective. I contemplated other degrees. Switching majors would certainly mean staying longer than the four years I had planned and I didn't have the money for that. What did I really want to do with my life? At 20 years old, I didn't have the answer to that important question, but at least I could start eliminating things. Lawyer? Nope. FBI agent? I don't think so. Dentist? Not a chance. I figured I needed to go a little broader to open up my options.

Thinking back a few years, I'd always been interested in being my own boss, but didn't really correlate that to being business minded. I remembered working for a very small lawn mowing company; just the owner and me. I was always thinking about how I would have done things differently. We didn't wear uniforms. I would have had us wearing shirts emblazoned with the company logo. I would have put the logo on a decal on the company truck too. I don't think he even had a logo. He didn't do any marketing either. I actually went home and made flyers for my own make-believe lawn mowing business; as if I owned the company. *Tyler's Lawn Care. Give your lawn a little TLC!* Corny, I know.

As I looked back, it made me think that I was more interested in business and marketing. I wanted to build and create companies. Be my own boss. Of course, I wished I would have just gone straight into a business degree. But I hadn't and I needed to figure this out.

I decided to go talk to the assistant dean of the business school at the University of Washington where I was going to school. I had never stepped foot in a business building on campus. I told him my story as well as not wanting to go back and start over with a business degree. He asked if I'd done any internships or apprenticeships. I hadn't. If I could get some internships and show future employers that I'd had some business experience, this would at least show that I was moving in the right direction, even with a political science degree. He said it would also help me build my network. I didn't completely understand what that meant or the importance of it yet, but I was willing to do it.

I reached out to a friend who was working for one of the first digital advertising agencies in Seattle. He got me an internship doing sales and marketing on a project called Seattle Square. It was a shopping experience for Seattle area businesses. I went door to door trying to convince these small stores they should have a one page website on SeattleSquare.com. The experience taught me a lot about hard work and persistence, but more than anything, it introduced me to the business of the Internet. Building web sites, creating online ads and eCommerce. This was the mid 1990s and the world wide web was just getting going. It was the first time I recognized something I was really passionate about. I LOVED the Internet. I loved how it could connect businesses with its customers and convey all the things they needed to help sell their products and services, way more than any printed billboard or brochure could do. It was interactive, engaging and certainly the way of the future. I was hooked.

Having that internship on my resume helped me get a summer job in the marketing department of a large manufacturing company coordinating the design and development of their first corporate website. It was a dream come true and helped me get valuable experience on my resume. The relationships I formed at that company allowed me to get a full-time job with them after graduation. I went back to the marketing department helping manage the website and all online communications. I fell in love with this work and it was the start to my career in digital marketing.

After working at a number of companies and learning a lot along the way, it was finally time to honor my entrepreneurial interests, follow my passions and start my own firm. I partnered with a colleague and we created our first company Seven2, a digital creative advertising agency. I was scared as could be. My wife and I had two small kids at home, we'd taken a large loan against our house to start the business and no guarantee that this was actually going to succeed.

Thankfully, due to a lot of hard work, amazing co-workers and the support of our families, over the years we've created thousands of websites, ads, online games, social media campaigns and videos for some of the biggest brands in the world including AT&T, Amazon, Nintendo, Netflix, Disney, MTV and many others. A few years later, we started another digital advertising agency called 14Four. Then became partners in a digital media buying company called Strategy Labs. Having other aspirations outside of digital marketing, we also opened three juice bars called Method Juice Cafe and two yoga/spin/TRX gyms called The Union.

Over the years, I've been fortunate enough to discover and live out my affinity for digital marketing, entrepreneurship and volunteer work. They have all brought me great fulfillment and happiness.

You will hear my voice in these pages come through C.J., the mentor. We share a love for inspiring others to dream big, align with their unique skills and interests and live out their passions. There is no greater joy than seeing someone do just that.

This book tells a story of someone who is pursuing a four year college degree. But that is only one journey. Yours might be attending a two year community college, a trade school or jumping right into the workforce. Either way, the techniques laid out in this book can be employed in all of those scenarios.

It is my hope that this book is the compass you need to chart your course with purposeful direction. That it's a megaphone for that inner voice that wants to shoot for the moon. And also a reminder to offer yourself some grace along the way. We're always learning, growing and becoming better versions of ourselves.

These things are already inside of you. It is your obligation to draw them out...and be more like you.

one

The Shot at the Buzzer

Three seconds on the game clock.

His team down 62-64 and the championship game on the line.

Rory Langford knew the ball was coming to him. He'd practiced this a million times in his mom's driveway to the play-by-play in his head.

Langford receives the inbound pass, the defender guarding him tight, stalking his every move, he fakes the drive toward the basket, steps back, creates space to get off a shot. Langford puts up a beautiful three pointer... It's a game-winning buzzer beater!

Now he took a deep breath. This was the real thing.

He leaned into the huddle and saw the tension in his teammate's faces. The last game of his senior season and they needed this win to go on to State.

Coach Lewis was calm as ever as he drew up the play. Rory felt a nervous thrill run through him, but he knew he was ready. He would get the last shot of the game.

He heard the noise of the home crowd. He felt the nervous smile of his mother there in the stands, and knew she was clutching her lucky charm and cheering him on. He felt the brown eyes of Emma watching him.

"Blue Devils on three!" said Coach.

The other players grinned at Rory.

"One, two, three, Blue Devils!"

Focus. Focus. Focus. You know what to do.

Everything went into slow motion. Rory heard the ref's whistle. He felt the weight and texture of the basketball between his hands.

There was Jevon with the screen, and Brandon, the inside big man, scrambling open. Rory inbounded to Brandon, ran to his side, took the ball and dribbled left. A defender came at him. Rory jumped and released. In that beautiful moment, there was no crowd, no sound, no other players, not even Emma. Just a ball and a hoop, suspended in time.

As the ball arced through space, the buzzer sounded and the crowd seemed to take one gigantic gasp.

Rory watched, waited, hoped.

His final shot hit the rim and flew wide.

He felt the emotions flood his young body as he stood there and the opposing players began their celebration. It all seemed surreal. Teammates began patting him on the back. He made eye contact with Emma across the gym, and she just shook her head and walked away.

No good.

Game on the line and you blew it.

No second chance.

All those days of basketball, starting at the YMCA when he was five. Traveling and playing on the road. Being the star point guard at legendary Jefferson Heights in front of a packed gym at home games. Early morning practices, after school practices, weight room practices, film practices.

And what did it all mean now?

He knew he'd never play in the NBA, knew the daunting numbers by heart. Just over three percent of high school players get to play on a college team and just over one percent of those players make the NBA.

It wasn't going to happen. He knew he would never compete in this way again. There was a loss in that and he mourned it, even as the celebration continued around him in that high school gym. The lights began to blur with his tears.

"You were amazing," said the best voice in the world.

It was Mom, wrapping him up in her arms, encouraging him as she had done since his very first game.

"You did your best, son. I'm so proud of you."

His tears came a little faster. He'd wanted to win the game for her, and to be honest, for Emma too. He remembered all the times Mom had driven him to practice, washed his uniforms, shot hoops with him.

One special time, she'd taken him to watch his beloved Cleveland Cavaliers play the Los Angeles Clippers. Even with the nosebleed seats they'd been able to afford, Rory was electrified. He loved the enormity of the arena, the energy in the place. It was the real thing.

As Rory sat in the locker room, still trying to absorb the loss, he saw three texts from Emma.

Hey you, tough game, sorry.

Totally lost my voice screaming for you guys tonight.

Been thinking & guess I wanna just be friends for now. -Em

He tried calling and texting her back and got no reply.

It was the worst day of his young life.

/ two /

Shadows of Doubt

"I just can't get fired up about calculating the seismic risks of a 48-story building," Rory told his college roommate, Xavier. They sat on a bench on the college campus, demolishing lunch from the Tacos Grande food truck.

Rory the heartbroken star point guard had become Rory the slightly confused college student. He picked a good school, Payton University, and did his best to choose a good degree. Civil engineering seemed a decent fit. Mom always said he was an expert at putting things back together.

"Why'd you pick that major, anyway?" Xavier asked.

"Truth is, I have no clue what I want to do in life, let alone major in," Rory said. "I'm certainly up for suggestions."

"No idea, huh?"

"No idea. It seems crazy we have to graduate high school, not knowing anything about the professional world, then pick a college known for the field we want to major in."

"Right?"

"Then, hinge everything on this major hoping to find a job. Wondering if it's going to mean happiness or misery."

"The gap year sort of makes sense," Xavier said. "You know, that thing they do in Europe where you take some time off, volunteer, travel, whatever, take a break."

"It makes a lot of sense," Rory said. "Except I know it's hard for Mom sending me to school as it is. I can't see her excited about a gap year."

"Probably not."

"I should have saved more from my summer job. I made three grand mowing lawns, but I spent it on going out and on that new stereo for my car."

"Gotta admit that bass sounds pretty sweet though," Xavier said.

"What about you?" Rory said. "How did you figure it out?"

"Well, I figured out what I didn't want to do," Xavier said. "I did a job shadow."

"You were thinking about law?"

"Yeah, so when I was in high school, I really thought I wanted to be a lawyer. They make tons of money. People seemed impressed when I talked about it."

"Job shadowing changed that?"

"My career counselor set it up and I spent a couple hours with this lawyer. He was super nice and all, but wow, that job was boring."

"Really? I thought there'd be a little more action."

"That guy sits in his office all day on his computer," Xavier said. "He was either researching real estate law, writing contracts or sometimes dealing with land developers in court. Man, I don't know what I thought lawyers really did, but that did not sound like it fit me. I'm so glad I got a chance to talk with that guy and at least learn a bit more about the industry. Even if it meant changing my mind."

"Smart call," Rory said. "Listening to you, I realize I don't know anything about the day-to-day life of an engineer. And I'm spending a lot of time and money on this degree."

"Sounds like you need some help," Xavier said.

"I do. I need to take this more seriously but I don't know where to turn. I need a plan."

three

Meeting a Mentor

"Your mom says you're trying to figure some things out."

C.J. Parker, his mom's high school friend, had kind eyes. She was dressed to perfection and her office, high in a downtown office building, seemed right out of a movie set. Glass walls, white leather chairs, an assistant offering coffee and bottled water. C.J. clearly seemed to be someone who had breezed through school and chased exactly what she wanted. It was hard not to envy that right now.

"I guess I do need to figure it out," Rory said. His palms were damp and his voice sounded quavery to him in the big office. "By the way, Mom says hi. Every time she talks about you it's an award you won, or another company you started. She's pretty much in awe."

"Well, I'm in awe of your mother," C.J. said. "And she has some pretty great things to say about you."

Rory straightened up in his chair a little.

"How's school going?" C.J. asked. "Sophomore, right?"

"Yeah, civil engineering. It's okay, I guess. I do love Payton. People are great and I love watching football and basketball.

But I'm not so sure I'm on the right track. Engineering is just… it's just not any fun."

"I understand that feeling," C.J. said. "Did you know I was a psychology major?"

"Really?"

"I thought I wanted to be a detective or a crime scene investigator. That meant a psychology or criminal justice degree. That was the track I was on."

Rory looked out past the glass wall at dozens of her employees beyond. "This looks a long way from the police beat," he said.

"I was actually a little further in school then you are now, and I really started to ask myself if this was something I wanted to do. The more I thought about it, I really couldn't see myself working in law enforcement. People talk about the late nights and emotional strain. That didn't really sound like me. I realized I was going to waste years and money on school I wasn't going to use."

Rory was all ears. This was sounding quite familiar.

"But weren't you pretty far along in your psychology degree by then? Did you consider changing majors?"

"I did. But that would have meant retooling my whole major and probably adding on a year or two more of school. So I found another solution."

"This is exactly what I need to hear," Rory said. He leaned forward. "How did you do it?"

Just then, C.J.'s phone buzzed multiple times and she glanced down.

"I can't wait to tell you." she said as a frustrated look began to form across her face. "But right now, I have to take care of a client emergency. I'm so sorry to have to cut our meeting short."

Bummer. So close.

She stood up and offered a handshake.

"How would you feel if we meet again soon?" C.J. asked. "I have something in mind that can help you figure out your own path. A way to navigate from school to job and do what you really want to do."

"That sounds amazing," Rory said, and shook her hand.

"Again, so sorry about that. Please see my assistant on the way out to schedule our next meeting," C.J. said. "Have a great day, Rory."

He went out through the office spaces humming with activity. People grouped around a laptop exchanging ideas. Others with headphones working away. They all looked engaged, focused and happy. The feeling he remembered from the basketball court. He wanted that again.

Thanks to C.J., he felt like he was walking a little taller already. He wished Emma could see him now.

/ four /

Where Circles Join

Three weeks later, C.J. waited in her office for the kid to come back. She looked forward to seeing him again. Her friend's only son. She'd seen him grow up in a series of Christmas cards and in her friend's occasional stories. She knew Rory was a good kid, but apart from basketball had never quite found the place he fit in.

And that sounded all too familiar, the youthful quest for purpose. In a way, her own journey seemed like yesterday, but again, it seemed like ages ago she had started her own working life. She remembered the frustration of working for someone else and the fear of finally striking out on her own. The thrill of the first big deal. The satisfaction of joining with partners in a common goal. Celebrating company milestones. Hard to believe in some ways the companies she owned today: An executive recruiting firm with clients like Starbucks, United Way and Target, a human resources software company and a chain of bootcamp gyms.

And now here at her office door was Rory, with that shy grin and lanky frame.

"Rory, it's great to see you," she said. "How have you been?"

"Hey, nice to see you too. I can't lie, I've been excited about getting back together and hearing more about your story. I even did a little research on you."

"Yes? I hope you didn't find the elusive photo of me at a pie-eating contest for a local non-profit fundraiser," C.J. said. "It's a good one."

"Haha, no, but I might have to look later," Rory said. They both laughed.

"So you told me last time you decided being a detective might not work for you," Rory said. "I really want to hear more about that. Like I said, I'm not so sure this civil engineering track is right for me."

"Ah yes," she said, getting back into it. "That was a little scary. I was in the middle of my junior year and had already taken a lot of psychology classes. I really didn't want to go back and start taking new classes in a new major."

"So what did you do?"

"Well, I started to look at myself a little more closely. Strangely, I hadn't really done that yet."

"What do you mean?"

"I began to ask myself, what was I truly interested in? What kind of things were more aligned with my innate skills and interests? What was I passionate about? It really wasn't crime scenes and law enforcement. So what kind of person was I? I remembered that during high school, I'd taken some DECA classes and really loved them."

"What's DECA?" Rory asked.

"Our high school had these business classes where we could compete on topics like marketing, finance and management. I even made it to the state level. I didn't really think of it as a possible career. I just enjoyed the classes and they felt like an easy credit."

"Nice."

"But when I started to look back on high school and what classes I really enjoyed and excelled in, I remembered how much I loved those DECA classes. It made me think maybe I was more interested in business and marketing. The challenge of building and growing companies seemed really interesting. To be my own boss."

C.J. smiled as she said this. She could still feel that early flush of excitement.

"Of course, I wished I would have just gone straight into a business degree. But I hadn't and now I needed a new path forward."

"So what did you do?" Rory asked. This sounded very familiar.

"My Dad gave me the names of two of his friends who were in business, and I called them to ask some questions. I remember asking if my psychology degree was going to be a problem. They both said it was fine, but I would need to show I was serious about business. They said job shadows and internships would be important and that they would also help me build my network. I didn't completely understand what that meant, but I was willing to do it."

"Interesting," Rory said. "My friend Xavier was just telling me about job shadowing."

"Did he try it?"

"Yeah, it made him realize he actually *didn't* want to be a lawyer."

"Well that can be just as important when figuring things out," C.J. said. "So in my case, I took the advice, stuck with my psychology degree and got some great internships."

"Wow, interesting," said Rory. "I know it worked out really well for you." He looked keen but also confused. "So...what do you think I should do?"

"I thought you'd never ask," C.J. said, and they both laughed again. "Actually, Rory, the great thing is, you're going to be able to answer that for yourself."

"I am?"

"Yes, and I'm going to show you how."

C.J. pointed to her wall.

"That is my Ikigai diagram," she said. The framed image showed four neatly drawn intersecting circles. Rory leaned forward for a closer look.

"The Western interpretation of Ikigai is a blending of four ideals," C.J. told him. "What you're good at, what you love, what the world needs and what you can get paid for. A great friend gave me this, and it has a great deal of meaning to me. I put it up there as a reminder for all my pursuits."

Rory looked at that word in the center, where all four circles came together. IKIGAI.

"It's a Japanese concept that means *reason for being*," C.J. said. "It's seen as a way of creating a life not only fulfilling and meaningful, but also long and healthy. Doesn't that sound wonderful?"

"It's exactly what I want," Rory said. "And I've got no idea how to get there."

five

A Friendly Game of Horse

"Let's walk," C.J. said. "Sometimes when you're feeling stuck, movement is the best thing. Let me show you the loft."

She pointed Rory up the stairs and followed him.

She was proud of the loft, another way of taking good care of the people who worked for her. Rory looked surprised to see couches, a foosball table and a few old-school arcade machines.

"No way," he said.

She grinned.

"This is where some of my best ideas happen," she said. "Either here, or in our gym."

"You have your own gym here?" Rory seemed in awe.

"Isn't it great? My partners and I really value physical and mental health. And seriously, movement means creativity as far as I'm concerned."

She grabbed a nerf basketball and shot it straight at Rory's chest.

"Ok, you and me, game of horse." She pointed at the hoop on the wall.

Rory smiled and took his shot. He instantly looked more at ease.

She matched his next two shots and missed the third. She was up against the star Blue Devils point guard, after all.

"H for me," she said. "Okay, question for you, Rory. Say you won the lottery and didn't have to worry about finding a job that made you enough money, what would you do with your time?"

"Anything?"

Rory missed his jump shot.

"Yeah, anything. And you can't just say you'd lie around and do nothing, because we both know you'd be doing something." C.J. made her shot with a swish. "Imagine anything. Picture tons of money to do whatever you wanted."

Rory stepped to where she had been and hesitated. "Honestly, I don't know."

"That's actually a normal response," C.J. said. "Most of us haven't taken the time to stop and ask what we truly would do with all the time and money in the world."

"It's completely unrealistic," Rory said. "I'll never have unlimited amounts of money." He took his shot and missed. "H here."

C.J. said. "C'mon, where's your imagination?"

She stepped up and made another basket.

Rory missed again.

"Hey, no fair, home court advantage," he said. "HO for me. And I do have an imagination."

"Just kidding," C.J. said. "But really, it's meant to get you thinking about the kinds of things you like to do no matter how unrealistic they seem. Obviously, we gravitate toward activities we find interesting or fun. And when we're doing things we find fun, we tend to be happier. And that's kind of the whole point, right?"

They both made their next shot.

"You know, I never looked at it that way before," Rory said. "I always thought you're just supposed to pick your major, get a degree and then find a job so you can make enough money to pay your own bills. Basically, become independent then hope you kind of like your job. Right?"

C.J. smiled. This could have been her 20-year-old self talking.

"I get it. I thought the same thing growing up. The problem is it becomes more transactional. A means to an end. And not really something that leads to a career that makes you happy. Don't get me wrong, you have to pay the bills. But why not try and be a little more intentional about finding something that truly utilizes your unique skills and interests. When you leverage those talents, in an industry you find interesting, you tend to have more joy in your work. Contrary to popular belief, Rory, work doesn't have to feel like...well...work."

Rory laughed and made a long shot from the corner.

"You're up," he said.

Even in a game of horse with a nerf ball, C.J. felt the competitive rush. She loved that feeling and felt it flow through her veins with appreciation, even as her shot went wide.

"Those people down there?" she pointed below. "My employees? They are right in the center of those circles I showed you. That Ikigai space."

Rory took her pass and leaned over the railings to look below. There was a productive hum in that big place.

"It must feel amazing," he said.

"It does!"

"Then help me find that," Rory said.

"I would absolutely love to," C.J. said.

They looked at each other, grinning, the game forgotten for now.

"Trust me," she said. "When you align yourself with what you're good at and what you're passionate about, you're truly unstoppable. You're creative. You're focused. You're happy."

"Sign me up!"

"So... what you're really trying to do is be more like you."

Be more like you. Rory thought those were some of the wisest words he'd ever heard. So simple but it made so much sense.

"You're already on your way," C.J. said. "We're going to find out what your strengths are and what kind of things give you life. You're going to find a career path that truly aligns *your* particular skills and interests, one that will bring you more happiness and fulfillment. That's what you want, right?"

"I'm ready!"

She picked up a remote from the coffee table and a big screen TV on the wall came to life.

"Come check this out," she said.

She sank into a comfortable chair and Rory did the same.

"Are you okay on time?" C.J. asked. "Any engineering classes you're missing to be here?" She winked at him.

"No, I mean, yes, but I should be asking you," Rory said. "Mom told me what you bill by the hour and I am taking a lot of your afternoon."

C.J. smiled and Rory saw the kindness behind those eyes again.

"No, there will not be a bill," she said. "And yes, I value my time very highly, but that's even more reason to spend it with you this afternoon. A good person once helped me very much along my own path, and it's my pleasure to pay that favor forward.

"And now," she said, "I'm going to show you the really good part."

/ six /

The Art of Introspection

C.J. pressed a button and the TV screen filled with five words:

Introspection
Design
Exploration
Adaptability
Service

"The IDEAS Framework is my gift to you," she said. "It's a system I built to help you succeed."

Rory already felt like a different person than the one who had walked rather timidly into this intimidating office an hour ago. He had forgotten his anxieties about seismic risk and calculus. He twirled the nerf ball in his hands as he sat there and it gave him comfort. His head was spinning but in the best of ways.

"These are five steps in the journey to finding alignment and happiness," he heard C.J. say. "Each step requires work on your part, but each will get you closer to answering that big question: What do I want to do with my life and how do I get there?"

"Wow!" Rory said. "And you came up with this?"

"Over the years I've helped a lot of students," she said. "I love seeing them take the time to uncover their own unique skills and interests, identify industries they're passionate about and begin building connections and learning experiences that will help them along the way."

"I love how… how… intentional you are with this," Rory said, finding the word. "And how you're helping others."

"Believe me, I get a lot of fulfillment and purpose from giving back," C.J. said. "I'll explain all about that as we go. It's actually part of the framework."

"Of course it is." Rory said, nodding and smiling.

"So here's the deal," C.J. said. "Before our next time together, I want you to focus on the first step, which is Introspection."

"Introspection? Self-examination? Reflection?" Rory asked. "Yeah, I won't lie, I'm not so great at that."

"Honestly, none of us really are. And we usually don't take the time to truly understand ourselves. For that very reason, so many people end up taking a professional path that doesn't really align with who they are. It ends up causing friction their entire career."

Rory thought about his Uncle Chris who always complained about his job and never seemed very happy. Maybe a little self-reflection couldn't hurt, after all.

"Just imagine if you actually took the time to uncover a few things about yourself and used that awareness to guide your journey," C.J. said. "Have you ever taken a personality test?"

Rory shook his head.

"Ok, I want you to learn a bit about your own personality. And testing allows you to get it down on paper and review your findings. You can look at the results, agree or disagree with what they say and start to analyze yourself a bit more."

"Okay, I'm game."

"There are a couple things to be aware of. One, you have to be open-minded to the results. At first, you might not agree with some of what they say because of the view you've held about yourself all these years. Just be open to learning some new things. Second, these tests are in no way definitive in explaining who you are. They're meant to quickly help you gain insights on how you see and approach the world. You can always spend more money if you want to in order to get professional consultation about your results and for some people this can be really useful, but it's not necessary."

"It sounds really interesting."

"I suggest searching the internet for two personality tests. The first is referred to as the 16 personalities or Myers-Briggs test. The other is the Enneagram personality test. There are a number of free tests online that will give you results after taking 10 to 15 minutes to fill out the questionnaire. They both have a little different perspective, but it's interesting to compare and contrast your results from each test. And if you're really feeling ambitious, check out CliftonStrengths, formerly StrengthsFinder, to learn a little more."

Rory pulled out his phone to take some notes.

"Ah, don't worry, I'll send you all this in an email," C.J. said.

"Oh good!" Rory said. "You know, I've never considered taking one of these tests. But now I'm kind of interested in what they would say."

"It can be pretty fun and I think you'll enjoy analyzing the results."

"I'll definitely check them out."

"Great," C.J. said. "Then comes part two of Introspection. Once you know more about your personality, I need you to hone in on where your interests and passions lie."

Rory felt a little overwhelmed. And once again, he was amazed by C.J.'s kindness and perception.

She smiled and took a deep breath. He did the same.

"Let's take a quick break," she said. "You know your way around by now, so let's meet back in my office in 15 minutes."

She rose and flashed Rory that smile that made him feel like exactly the person he was meant to be.

/ seven /

The Winding Path

When he arrived back at her office, he was impressed once again to see C.J.'s shelves tidy, her desk swept clean, her attention focused completely on him.

"Look, Rory, here is the real key to Introspection," she said. "Simply put, what brings you joy? Tough question, I know. I have some questions that will help and I've just emailed them to you."

Focused, organized, efficient. No wonder this woman ran three successful companies, Rory thought.

"The question of joy is where most of us quickly self-sabotage," C.J. said. "It's harder to see the direct connection between our hypothetical areas of interest and a realistic, well-paying job."

"I can tell!"

"But don't worry. Just follow the process and it will all make sense. Take some time to sit down and really answer those questions. And don't limit yourself. Dream big!"

"I can't wait to get my hands on them," Rory said with a feeling of optimism.

"And I can't wait to see your answers," C.J. said. "We'll go over them together. You might be surprised. Most people look at their answers and right away try to find a job type. Our instinct is to match a job type with the real world and then question whether or not we can make money at that job. I want you to take one step back. Look again at your answers and start to identify the industries they're in. All of our passions and interests have industries around them. Oftentimes, multi-billion dollar industries with all sorts of jobs supporting them."

Multi-billion? Rory liked the sound of that.

"Take the statement, 'If money was no object, I'd travel the world.' Obviously there is a passion for travel and adventure there. Quickly we dismiss it, because we don't think we can make any money at it. Usually that's because we don't know anyone who has. But why not investigate that more? You could work for an airline, become a travel writer, become a host with a travel tour company or be a global hotel inspector. A quick search will produce all sorts of options in your passion industry. Likely jobs you'd never thought of. Then you can start to look at those jobs and see what sounds like you, utilizing your personality traits and skills. When you find a couple, you can research the requirements those jobs might have like schooling, certifications, internships or apprenticeships. It's so much better to start with an industry you're passionate about and then look at the jobs in that industry. How great would it be to wake up every day and go to work in an industry you love?"

"It would be amazing," Rory said. "So, how did you land on the industry you're passionate about?"

"Well honestly, my approach at the time was a little different."

"Really?"

"I know, right? I wish I would have taken the time to stop and really thought about what industry I was passionate about. Who knows, maybe now I'd be in the music industry if I had."

"Music, huh?" There were more and more interesting levels to this woman in front of him.

"Instead, I did what a lot of people do. As per the advice from the assistant dean of the business school, I started looking for an internship and ended up taking the first one I could get. I had a friend who was a couple years older than me and was already working in business. I went to him to see if his company had any internship openings. They were a recruiting and staffing firm in the tech industry that helped companies find new employees."

"Ah."

"Now I already told you that internships/apprenticeships are incredibly valuable, but my mentality at the time was that I just needed *any* internship I could get. Well little did I know, but I found recruiting really fascinating. I loved creating relationships with people and helping them find a job that really fit them. This was way before anything like LinkedIn."

It must have been the look on his face that made C.J. laugh.

"You're trying to calculate how old I am. That probably sounds like a long time ago to you."

"No, no, not at all." Rory said.

"So for me, it was a little bit of dumb luck that my first internship, while trying to find any business opportunity I could get, ended up being in a field I fell in love with. That certainly doesn't always happen."

"That's pretty lucky."

"It is, but it also demonstrates another one of my philosophies. Just like your friend Xavier, I could have done the internship and really disliked the experience and thought it was a waste of time. But that's not true. Time and again, I've seen students get a lot of anxiety by thinking they have to pick the exact right internship. Or even the exact right major or career from day one. That's really hard to do. Introspection helps you narrow down your skills, interests and industries so that you're pointed in the right direction, but you still have to be adaptable and willing to learn and grow. And you have to be okay with the winding path."

"The winding path?"

"Yes, so often we want a straight line to the perfect major, job shadow, internship and career. We don't want to make any mistakes along the way. But we'd be happier if we could just shift our perspective. If we could look at every opportunity as a learning experience and not a failure. I've learned something very important: There is no losing, just learning."

"Yes," Rory said. He thought about that three-pointer he'd missed at the buzzer. What had he learned that day?

"As you look back at your efforts, it never looks like a straight course," C.J. said. "The best experience and knowledge comes from the winding path."

The winding path. It was a fascinating thought. All his young life, he'd felt the pressure to make the shot, to win the game, to make all the right moves. He'd never considered that losing might be learning. It was a lot to think about at once.

Once again it seemed like C.J. could read his mind.

"Ok, that's enough of that," she said. "I've given you plenty to chew on, haven't I?"

Rory exhaled.

"Let's do this," she said. "Take Introspection as far as you can for the next four weeks. I really think it's going to unlock some clues for you. When we get back together, we'll talk it all through."

His head was buzzing with more excitement and confidence than he'd felt in a year.

"I absolutely can't wait," he said.

"Let me leave you with this," C.J. said on his way out. "I said it before, but I'll say it again. Dream big. Don't limit yourself. People spend their childhood passionate about things like sports, music or dance and then don't pursue it later in life because they don't think they can make a living at it. They say things like 'I'll never make it as a pro snowboarder' or 'I'm not good enough to get my own record deal.' That might be true, but there are whole industries around those aspirations that could be incredibly rewarding and fulfill who they are as a person."

"So you're telling me to find those childhood dreams," Rory said.

"Absolutely. There's a reason for that passion. There's something inside us that loves to be a part of those pursuits. The snowboarder could work in manufacturing at a snowboard company or be an instructor for young kids. The musician could be a promoter for a record company, an artist manager or music industry attorney. The point is, just because you can't be at the very top, don't give up on that dream."

Steps to Take

(Bits of wisdom to reinforce concepts from the book and help you carry out the IDEAS Framework.)

- Go to www.bemorelikeyou.com/workbook and download the IDEAS Framework workbook.

- Take the personality tests and study the results. Know yourself.

- Answer the Industry Mapping questions (next page). What recurring answers do you see? What industries keep coming up?

- Be ok with the winding path. There is no "right" way.
- There is no losing, just learning. Every experience builds on the previous.

- First, think about the industry around your passion. Then think about and research specific jobs in that industry.

- Don't give up on the dream. There is a reason you gravitated toward those activities that excite you. Explore them.

Industry Mapping Questions

1. What activities give you energy and excitement? When you're doing them, you lose track of time. When you're not doing them, you get excited thinking about the next time you will.

2. If you only had one month to live, and all the money in the world, what would you do? How would you spend your time? What would truly bring you joy?

3. When you were a kid, what did you always dream of doing as a job? Is that still interesting today? Why or why not?

4. If you could start a business or career tomorrow and guarantee success, what would you do?

5. What job always felt unrealistic or out of reach?

6. What do you do for fun in your spare time?

7. What classes did you enjoy in high school? What skills did they utilize?

8. Ask three different people what they could see you doing for a job and why.

9. What attributes do they see in you that apply to those types of jobs?

10. What are your five favorite accounts on social media or podcasts that you follow (aside from humor and famous people)? Why?

/ eight /

All a Waste of Time?

"Hey, whatcha reading there, roomie?"

Rory looked up to see Xavier grinning at him. He'd been totally engrossed in the book.

"It's called *Range* by David Epstein," Rory said. "It's fascinating."

"That doesn't look like an engineering textbook," Xavier said, slouching down onto the couch beside him.

"C.J. loaned it to me. Part of her master plan to help me find my path in life."

"That's awesome. At least someone is looking out for you." Xavier said. "So what's in the book?"

"Wow, so much," Rory said. "He talks about finding your job fit. He talks about the value of having lots of work experiences to draw from. You can sample different jobs to find what you like, while learning and becoming more proficient along the way."

"Makes sense."

"So as you take on new opportunities early in your professional life, you're learning new skills, new problems to solve and create new perspectives you can draw from to help you hone in on what it is you really want to do. This allows you to really know yourself and your skills and then go deep on something you really love and become really good at."

"Well put," Xavier said. "This lady C.J. really sounds like she's helping you."

"She's amazing," Rory said. "I look forward to introducing you someday soon. And yes, she's got my head buzzing with new ideas."

"Anything I'd appreciate?"

"For sure. Check this out." Rory grabbed his phone. "So I took C.J.'s advice, went online and took this thing called the Enneagram personality test. It took me about 15 minutes to answer the questions."

"And… results are, you're a kick ass dude lucky to have the smartest, best-looking roommate ever."

"Ha, true, but wait till you see this." He handed Xavier the phone.

"So it said I'm a Type Eight, what they call The Challenger. Type Eights are assertive, strong and self-confident. They are straightforward, resourceful, protective and decisive."

"That's my man!"

"We Challengers earn our name because we love to take on challenges, and also allow opportunities for others to challenge themselves. Type Eights tend to be charismatic people who use their skills to lead others, whether in business, government, church or the military."

"It all sounds like you, pretty much to a T," Xavier said. "I know you lead others well and you love taking on new challenges. Most definitely straightforward and decisive. So... what's the downside of being a Challenger type?"

"Well spotted, sir," Rory said. "All good strengths come with weaknesses."

"Yes," Xavier began counting off on his fingers. "One, forgets to take out the trash; two, leaves his stuff all over the floor; three, still hopelessly in love with a girl who doesn't want him; four..."

"Guilty as charged," Rory said. "And still working on all that. But you're right, the need for independence can cause Eights to worry about being controlled by others and this can cause conflict. Because they work so hard, they can lose emotional connections to those closest to them and not understand why those people pull away or find their behavior detrimental. They build up their egos so they cannot be hurt by others and this can cause them to shut down or be hardened emotionally."

"So does the shoe fit?"

"Hate to admit it, but yeah. In high school my drive to win sometimes caused a rift with others. Now I can really see the importance in understanding your own weaknesses and how it can affect your relationships with others like a boss, co-worker or even a loved one. I've got to let that sink in. I'm also planning to take another test, the 16 Personalities by Meyers-Briggs."

"You are taking this seriously," Xavier said. "I'm impressed. Time for a break and some ice cream?"

"No can do," Rory said. "I'm meeting C.J. tomorrow and I promised I'd get one more thing done first. She's the kind of person you never want to disappoint."

He showed Xavier the second list of Industry Mapping questions she'd given him.

"Daaaang. That lady asks some deep ones."

"Right? And she's really opened my eyes up to something. If you love snowboarding, she says, you don't have to be a pro snowboarder to succeed and chase your dreams. Find something associated with snowboarding you're really good at. Same with music, or any other dreams."

"So where does that leave you, amigo?"

"Never thought about it," Rory said. "I always thought about how much money I could make or if the classes were hard or easy. I thought about your regular old jobs like lawyer, accountant or salesperson. I'll be honest, this C.J. is really challenging me. So I'll send you off for ice cream on your own, and I'm going to wander the streets and search for answers."

"Good luck," Xavier said. "Go get 'em."

So Rory wandered. He realized he thought best when he was moving. C.J. was right again. As he walked, he tried his very best to get outside his head, his regular thoughts, and to dream big.

He had all of C.J.'s Introspection Questions copied into Notes on his phone, and whenever a thought popped into his head, he thumbed that answer into his phone. He'd taken her good advice, and not limited himself. No idea was too crazy or unrealistic.

Rory kept walking without thought of time. The afternoon shadows stretched out. He didn't feel hunger, didn't feel restlessness. This is what it felt like to be all consumed by an idea or a project.

As evening came on, he had his answers about what mattered most in life. And that felt good. But reading back through them, they seemed a little disjointed, maybe a lot disjointed. He'd hoped maybe there would be a common direction. Instead, his list showed there were all kinds of things he was interested in in life. He'd taken C.J.'s advice, done his best to identify and list any kind of work he could think of related to those answers. Still, he just couldn't find a thread.

He was also lonely. Xavier was right. He still thought about Emma all the time. He'd messaged her and tried to call a few times. She never said much in return. Maybe if he had won that game, maybe if he had been better at everything, she would still be around.

Without realizing it, he followed a familiar sound, the comforting smack of a basketball against a court. In the dark, under the floodlights, a group of kids played a pick-up game. Rory sat in the bleachers and watched the hypnotic movement of the ball from player to player, from end to end of the court.

Not good enough. Missed at the buzzer again. No second chances.

What if this was all a waste of time? What if the personality tests, the lists, the books were a dead end? At that moment it all seemed like a fanciful dream. Instead, he should be studying engineering. The thought tightened his gut.

Back to reality, buddy. Pass the class, get the grade, find a job, make some money.

He shivered, and with his head hanging low, trudged through the dark to find that engineering textbook once again.

/ nine /

Back in the Game

This time, C.J. was standing up and prowling her office. She was frowning instead of her usual sunny smile.

"So, you stood me up," she said. "You're late."

Rory felt his stomach drop and his neck flush.

"I tried to call…"

"Rory, you're better than that," she said. "You know how I value my time and structure my day. I've been…"

It was the first time he'd seen her out of center. He was devastated.

She sat down and took a deep, slow breath. She smiled at him now.

"I'm having a difficult day, and I took it out on you," she said. "That's not fair."

"It's more than fair," Rory said. "I feel like a loser."

"You, my friend, are the farthest thing there is from a loser," C.J. said. Even when she was upset, it was amazing the power she had to make him feel better. "Now, instead of anger, understanding," she said. "I'll go first."

She looked at him with those penetrating eyes that seemed to see his soul.

"I haven't been taking time for self-care," she said. "I told you how important that is. But with a big client making demands, I've let it get to me. I'm not sleeping, eating or working out the way I usually do."

Rory was absolutely taken aback to hear his mentor talking so candidly.

"So I apologize for jumping down your throat," she said. "That's not like me."

"I did deserve it," Rory managed a half smile.

"Yes, so tell me." Those penetrating eyes again. "How is such a promising young lad late for a date with his own future?"

"I have a confession to make," Rory said in a small voice. "I almost didn't come today at all. I've been putting it off."

C.J.'s eyes flashed hurt but quickly recovered.

"And why is that?"

"I did the personality tests," Rory said. "I answered all your good questions. And at the end, I was more confused than before."

"Tell me more."

He told her about walking until dark, thinking and writing, about sitting, cold and hungry, on the bleachers watching some kids play a basketball game. He confessed his doubt and anxiety that all this was just a waste of time, that he should go back to engineering and quit thinking about it.

"Please don't be upset," Rory said. "I know you've spent a lot of time on me already, and I can't thank you enough. It might just not be meant to be."

She looked at him and didn't say anything. Then she broke into a mysterious half smile.

"So, you have a list after all," she said. "Well, let's see it."

Rory stammered and stuttered that his list hadn't been good enough to send her.

"You have it on your phone? Will you Airdrop it to me?"

Her phone beeped a second or two later. Her brow furrowed as she read.

"I see."

"Know what I mean? All over the place, right?"

"Maybe, maybe not..."

Rory sat, as confused as ever.

"So when you were in doubt about everything, you found yourself back at a basketball court," C.J. said. "Isn't that fascinating?"

"I guess," Rory said. "Just habit."

"And on your list, do you see any reasons why you might have been drawn to that game that night?"

"Always loved the game, sure, but never good enough," Rory said. "Just kind of quit thinking about it so I could go make some kind of living."

"Look at your list again." C.J. sounded excited all of a sudden. "What's the pattern here?"

He stared at the list on his phone.

"Things you tend to follow on social media? What makes you most happy when you're doing it? Stuff you're most interested in reading about?"

They looked at each other.

"BASKETBALL!" they said at the same time.

Then Rory shook his head.

"I don't know. Seems out of reach," he said. "Unrealistic. Intimidating if I'm honest. In the past now."

"Understandable. We do that to ourselves, too often. We limit what we think is achievable. When in reality, it's usually just we don't have enough information on that thing. When we have more information about something then it seems more familiar. More possible."

Rory could relate. If something felt scary or unattainable it was usually because he just didn't have enough information about it. If he'd only take the time to learn a bit more in times of uncertainty.

"So basketball, eh?" she asked with eagerness in her voice. All traces of her earlier disappointment seemed swept away.

"I guess it's true," Rory said, catching her excitement himself. "Since I was a little kid, it's been one of my favorite things. I love to be on the court, or in the stands or watching it on TV. I love the competition. And I *love* the gear. The shoes, the clothes, the balls. I follow all the best players on social media and watch the top recruit lists for high school and college. I watch hours and hours of YouTube videos of highlight reels, up and comers, classic matchups and trick shots."

"That's awesome," C.J. said. "Rory, I have to thank you for taking my day from blah to great. It's hard to describe the sense of joy I feel when people start to uncover and focus on truths within their own life and put the energy into recognizing what interests and excites them. It's certainly a different conversation than identifying what will simply pay the bills. I'm proud of you for not limiting your ideas. Sometimes it's hard to dream BIG."

"Thanks, but I guess I still don't see the point," Rory said. "It's always just been something I've done for fun. It's not like I'm good enough to go pro and I'm not so sure hanging out at the park and playing pick-up games the rest of my life is a legitimate nine-to-five job. And you know Mom, she is definitely not going to like the sound of it. Seems pretty aimless."

C.J. laughed. "Yes, I do know your mother. And no, you're probably right. As great as it would be to play basketball everyday, you've got to dig a little deeper. Remember, I said that once you identify the thing, or few things, that truly bring you joy, then you have to start researching that industry and better understand the opportunities and jobs within it."

"I remember."

"You mentioned you liked basketball. That's great and specific and a good place to start. Next, you need to step back and think a little more generally about the industry. You said you liked the game, the competition and the gear. Basketball, or even more broadly, the sports industry, is a multi-billion dollar industry with lots of different categories within it. There are so many different facets that make up the sports industry. There's pro sports, college sports and recreational sports. There's working for teams, working for media companies running podcasts and websites and working for gear manufacturers. There are agents for athletes and the lawyers who do their contracts."

C.J. was on a roll. "Not to mention youth sports, camps and training the next generation of athletes. There's sports tourism, events and retail and online selling of sports equipment and memorabilia." She stopped to take a breath. "Sorry, I was going on and on to make a point. I say this all to let you know that there are *SO* many different facets to the industry that you're passionate about when you stop to take a second and look at it. It's easy to think of the one or two things that come to mind, but when you do the research, you uncover all sorts of categories and subcategories within your passion that could lead to really cool professional opportunities."

Rory's brain was hurting and he wasn't even the one doing all the talking.

"I see what you mean," he said. "There really are a lot of possibilities in basketball after all. Like I said, I've always loved the gear. Seems like that part of the industry is exploding."

"Yes!" C.J. said. "Then start to think about all the different categories within basketball gear. There's designing, manufacturing, testing, marketing and selling them."

Rory had never really let his mind run like this to think about *ALL* the possibilities. He'd never thought of what it could look like to have a career in something fun.

"Crazy, right?" C.J. must have seen he was a little overwhelmed. "It just takes a little more digging to uncover some really cool opportunities that are more in line with your skills and interests. More like you."

Rory could feel the excitement in him grow as he thought about the possibilities. *How cool would it be to actually have a job in basketball?*

"Okay, let's recap," C.J. said. "So far you've done a good job taking time to compile your list of interests and we've talked through some of the options within those interests. You've narrowed it down to basketball and possibly more specifically the gear."

Rory nodded.

"That's great," C.J. said. "But what if you're wrong?"

Rory was stunned. *Wrong? Hadn't they taken the time to follow the process and uncover the things he was most passionate about and interested in?*

"What do you mean?"

"We're complex creatures. We have lots of different interests. Some deeply rooted, some fleeting. This could be a passing fad for you."

"But this is something I've loved my whole life," Rory said. "Basketball has been a part of me. This was part of the whole exercise right?"

"Yes, and I hear you. And I believe you, but now you have to validate it. Now you need to spend some time with people in the industry. See what it's all about. The day-to-day."

Rory thought back to what his friend Xavier had said about job shadowing with the lawyer.

"Getting into the industry and meeting with professionals will also allow you to ask questions and help you narrow down what part of it really interests you. Design, industrial, marketing, or whatever. Then you can start to figure out what exact job types you might be interested in doing."

"Wow, okay." Rory felt invigorated, the doubt of last night forgotten.

"These are the next two phases of the IDEAS Framework: Design and Exploration. Design is doing the research and creating a plan of who you should talk to in the industry. Exploration is actually taking the initiative to reach out, meet and talk to those people and learn about their specific work."

"Sounds like I have some more work to do," Rory said.

"And here's the thing," C.J. said. There was caution in her eyes. "You need to be okay with being wrong. Maybe the basketball industry isn't exactly right for you. You have to have the courage to put yourself out there, learn some new things, and find out if they truly align with you."

Rory listened with all his heart.

"You see, there is a major problem that can hinder the mindset and attitudes of young adults. Honestly, it can affect any of us at any time, but the older we get, the more we see through it. That problem is fear. The fear of making a mistake. The fear of disappointment. The fear of failure. I've talked to so many young adults who believe they have to make the exact right choice after high school, find the exact right major or vocational program and then line up the perfect job shadow and internship."

"I know exactly what you mean," Rory said.

"This fuels the fallacy that there is one perfect path we have to navigate in order to find success. This myth puts tremendous pressure on young adults and can contribute to undue anxiety and stress. Sometimes, so much so, that it can even lead to inaction, which just keeps them stuck in the same place. Research shows that those who have a growth mindset about learning from their experiences, which includes failures, will grow, change and adapt better and find greater success along their path. It's okay to fail or be wrong. This philosophy is widely taught in entrepreneurship. There is so much to learn from failure. Young adults need to recognize this also pertains to their professional journey. Remember, no losing, just learning."

Again, Rory thought of Xavier and his job shadow with the lawyer.

"That sounds tough," he said. "I hate making mistakes. I do see a lot of my friends who are just like me. They're not really sure what they want to do with their lives and they feel so helpless. Even the ones who had a plan seem so stressed out about making sure they don't slip up along the way. Every decision has to be perfect. They're miserable."

"Yes, it can be tough," C.J. said. "But it's not about focusing on mistakes. It's about learning things about yourself and the work you're doing now will help you down the winding path that leads to better professional job fit and ultimately happiness and fulfillment. It's important to take it slow, put in the effort and learn as much as you can along the way."

"You said something about a growth mindset. Can you explain a little more?"

"Sure. There is no doubt you will face adversity. Rejection, missteps and failure are regular parts of life. The perspective you adopt when dealing with them can have a tremendous impact on your chance of success and overall well being. Carol Dweck, a psychological researcher, wrote a book called *Mindset* explaining her findings. A fixed mindset believes your qualities are carved in stone and when you fail, you're at the end of your abilities. You believe you're either good at something or you're not. People with a fixed mindset tend to quickly give up when they face adversity. You can see how limiting this might be to one's potential."

"Absolutely."

"But a growth mindset is very different. It looks at failure as an opportunity to learn from and grow. People with a growth mindset believe effort and attitude determine their abilities. They believe they can learn anything they want and that feedback is constructive. You can see how this sets you up to persevere. Adopt the no losing, just learning mentality. With this mindset, adversity is temporary. You know that you possess the necessary skills and attitudes, or can learn them, to overcome and create success through hard work."

Rory nodded.

"So you have to ask yourself," C.J. said. "Which perspective will you let rule your thoughts and motivate your life's actions?"

"This is really hitting home," Rory said. "In high school basketball, I never thought I was a good free throw shooter. At first I had a fixed mindset and believed it wasn't one of my better skills. But then I changed my attitude, which motivated me to learn more and practice and I became one of the best free throw shooters in the league my senior year."

"Exactly. And that mindset can be applied to the journey of finding your professional job fit."

"Yes! That makes total sense. I'm back on track now."

"I'm so glad to hear that." C.J. said with a big smile on her face. "So let's recap the Introspection phase of the IDEAS framework. You've learned a bit more about yourself by taking some personality tests. Keep those findings handy and look at them every once in a while. It's good to be thinking of your traits when you start to look at job types and want to see if they align with you. But don't forget you are always growing and changing and with a growth mindset you can certainly develop new traits."

"I get it."

"Good. You've also answered the questions about identifying the industries you're passionate about. I'm proud of you for seeing the recurring theme of basketball and having the courage to learn more about it."

"Thanks. It feels a little scary, but I'm excited, too."

"Now, let's talk about what's next."

"I'm super stoked. I really want to keep the momentum going." Rory bounced up and down in his chair.

"The Design phase is about mapping out a plan. The Exploration phase is about executing that plan. Now that you've identified the industry you're interested in, there are three main objectives in the Design phase: One, learn about the variety of job types within your industry. Two, start to identify, connect with and build a network of people that can help you along this path. Three, create real world learning opportunities by lining up informational interviews, jobs shadows and internships."

"Wow," Rory said. "There's a lot to this Design phase."

"True" C.J. agreed, "Introspection and Design are big steps to getting you where you want to go in life. Take your time with these phases. I guarantee your hard work will pay off."

"Mom always said, 'Nothing worth having is easy,'" Rory said.

"She's a wise woman."

"But I trust you, C.J., and I trust your process. I really want to find fulfillment. I'll do the work."

"Good! So before our next meeting, I want you to do some research on job types in the industry. In the beginning, give yourself some latitude to look at all sorts of jobs in the basketball industry, not just equipment. You never know what might excite you. Start with the broader industry and get more specific as you go. Do some research on the brands you love."

"That sounds like fun."

"It really is. Look at the careers pages on their websites. What kind of jobs are they hiring for? Read the job descriptions so you can get a better idea of what those jobs do. Start to take notes on what sounds interesting and what doesn't. This will help you get a better picture of what types of jobs are out there."

"I can do that." Rory said. "Thanks so much for today, C.J. You're incredible. You pulled me out of the dumps and back on the path. And I'll never be late again."

"My pleasure, Rory," C.J. said. "You made my day quite a bit brighter, too. I'm really excited to hear what you learn and talk about what comes next. See you soon."

Rory couldn't help it. On his way out her door, he paused, mock-dribbled an imaginary ball, then spun and shot toward the corner of her office.

"Nothing but net," he said with a grin.

Rory went straight back to his dorm room and cracked open his laptop. He successfully resisted the temptation to look at Emma's social media or message her. Instead of sport scores, or his upcoming engineering project, he Googled "jobs in basketball." As he scrolled through all the search results, he felt a buzz of anticipation. His first click was "10 jobs that are a slam dunk for basketball fans." Those jobs were: referee, coach, broadcaster, statistician, translator, videographer, IT manager, social media manager, athletic trainer and graphic designer. Interesting. Definitely some things he'd never considered.

Then he searched "NBA careers." He found the NBA's official site describing what it was like to work in the NBA and the many opportunities in the league. Rory found a list of people who worked for the NBA and profiles on them and their jobs, including facilities, global partnerships, digital media, content, corporate services, human resources and legal.

Rory sat back and thought about it. He remembered C.J. saying that so many of these industries were multi-billion-dollar operations and the job opportunities were almost endless. Maybe some of those dollars could flow his direction.

He worked on his new quest until the early hours of the morning. He wasn't hungry and he wasn't tired.

His next search was "basketball jobs Ohio" to see what was available in his state. He saw postings for coaches at a local kids' summer sports camp, marketing and promotions for a local college team and an accounting job in the same athletic department.

Following C.J.'s advice, he checked out the websites for some of his favorite basketball brands, starting with their "Careers" section. He was thrilled to find these questions from his favorite apparel and shoe company:

What kind of career would you like to pursue?
- Troubleshooting technology issues?
- Achieving the company's profitability goals?
- Dreaming up new products?
- Reducing environmental impact with sustainable innovation?
- Planning events?
- Interacting directly with customers?
- Helping day-to-day operations run smoothly?
- Creating digital experiences, products or applications?
- Working with suppliers and materials?

For Rory, still sitting there in his dorm room in the early morning hours as Xavier slept, there was a feeling of belonging and a thrill he had not felt in quite some time. Basketball was not a dream after all. People like him were earning a great living doing what they loved to do.

So what if he didn't land his dream job right out of college. Maybe getting into the industry and making contacts along the way would help his chances of learning about the industry and keeping an eye out for awesome opportunities.

He finally closed his laptop, brushed his teeth and crawled into bed, and when he finally did sleep, he dreamed a little about Emma, and a lot about basketball.

Steps to Take

- Dream big. Don't limit your industry search because you think it's not attainable.

- Be willing to put in the time and energy to validate your findings and be ready to be wrong, too. You might decide to choose a different industry.

- Don't let fear creep in and change your mind. Success does not usually look like a straight line. Be okay with the winding path.

- Adopt a growth mindset. You have the ability to learn, change and grow through adversity.

- Take the time to research. You will see that there are lots of different job types out there in all sorts of industries.

- These efforts also help you uncover possible people and companies to reach out to to help you learn more about the industry.

- This research helps you become more familiar with the industry. Familiarity makes things feel more attainable.

- When things start to feel attainable and not so out of reach, it helps you get excited about the opportunities and build momentum in your efforts.

ten

Connections

Today, C.J. felt like she could take over the world.

A good night's sleep, a good session in the gym this morning, and life was hers for the taking. It was an amazing feeling she wished everyone could experience.

Her next appointment was Rory. All morning she'd been looking forward to their conversation. At the gym she'd found herself rehearsing what to say. If he stuck with it, this kid was definitely going places. She found she was really enjoying the process. Watching her IDEAS Framework work its magic. Seeing the beginnings of a young career take shape.

"C.J., your ten o'clock is here," her assistant buzzed.

Wow, 10 minutes early. Rory, way to go! She smiled to herself.

As he strode into her office, there seemed to be a new purpose in his step. He reached out and shook her hand.

"You're early," she said.

"I promised you, never late again."

"And you dressed up."

"I found a clean shirt," Rory grinned.

"Well, you look sharp, and I'm impressed you're on time," C.J. said.

"And how are you doing today?" Rory asked her, looking her in the eyes.

"Great, thank you."

"No, I mean, really, how are you doing? After our last talk, I know you were having some challenges with self-care."

What a kid. That was always a good sign, when people started thinking outside themselves.

"Thank you, Rory, that's very considerate of you. I'm happy to report that life is good. We dealt with the client issue, and I'm sleeping and working out again. Much better. Now, enough about me. How did your research go?"

"It was actually pretty great." Rory said. "I didn't realize how many job types in the basketball industry were really out there. I feel kind of foolish for thinking that being a pro player was the only option."

"It's pretty cool, huh? So many jobs go into making all of these industries function. I hope some of the job types you saw resonated with you and the work you did in the Introspection phase. Remember, you want to be looking back at your personality traits and think of them when you're looking at descriptions of jobs you're interested in. This helps with finding alignment."

"That makes perfect sense."

"Remember, the Design phase is helping you identify not only the job types you might be interested in, but the people that can help be a resource along the way. This networking can help move you further down the path."

"Right," Rory said. "My high school marketing teacher Mr. Thomas always liked to say, 'It's not always what you know, but who you know."

"Absolutely right." C.J. said. "It's so important to start to grow your own network. Some of the people I met early in my journey are still friends and resources today. Your network can be a really strong tool for your lifelong career success."

"Fair enough," Rory said. "What do I need to do?"

"You start by asking everyone you know if they have any connections to your industry. Think about your mom, aunts, uncles, friends' parents, past teachers and current professors. Really, anybody in your current network. Let them know what you're up to. Do they have any connections in the basketball industry that they might introduce you to? These people are within your network and can possibly be links to the industry. Of course, this doesn't always work. We don't all have a vast network of people with deep connections, but it's the best place to start, and you have to start somewhere, right?"

"Actually, my friend Jeff's dad is a referee for college basketball games. I wonder who he knows?"

"Exactly," C.J. agreed. "Ask him! And think of who else you might know."

"I've got my work cut out for me now," Rory said.

"Yes, making connections takes effort, but I see it almost more like a game. Those connections can lead in all kinds of interesting directions. Who knows what you might uncover, and how awesome it might be. It just might be that next person you ask."

"I like the game idea," Rory said. "That perspective makes it a little more fun. But it seems like I'm going to run out of people I know pretty quick."

"How much do you know about LinkedIn?"

"It's a social network for professionals, right? Not really my thing, I'm more of an Instagram guy."

"It is. People post their professional profile on the site. Kind of like a beefed-up resume. You do have a resume right?"

Rory looked down. "Uh, no, I really haven't put anything together."

"Well, it's important to start. You can even begin by creating your LinkedIn profile and export it as a resume if you need a physical copy."

"Aye aye, mission accepted." Rory thumbed a reminder into his phone.

"It's a really important way to start building your network," C.J. said.

"I've got lots of friends."

"Can any of them get you an internship at a basketball equipment manufacturer?"

"Well, no, probably not." They both laughed.

"So, the point of building your network is to make some connections with professionals that can help you as you seek to better understand the industry and job type you're passionate about. Think of it as initial pathways to information, job shadows, internships/apprenticeships and even a real job someday."

"Those are all the things I need," Rory said. "Time to get to work."

"Once you get your own LinkedIn profile together, you can start to build your network by reaching out to people on the site. I do believe there is a right way of going about it though. Some people try to connect with everyone they possibly can. This is more of a scattered approach, and I wouldn't suggest it."

"But you never know who might be able to help you in the future. Why not connect with everyone?"

"True, but think about this. You have zero connection or context with those people. If someone else saw you were connected with them and wanted you to make an introduction, you really don't have any information or relationship with those people. They also don't have any reason to help you. Here's another way to look at it. Your virtual connections on

LinkedIn should be every bit as genuine or authentic as you'd want in the physical world."

"You make a very good point," Rory said.

"Of course, take any approach you want. I'm just telling you what's worked well for me."

"I'm definitely following your lead. So how do I start? Who do I reach out to?"

"Start with people you know like your relatives, family friends and professors. Early on, you might not get direct connections that can help you, but those people might be connected to others, in the industries you're looking for, and might make introductions for you. It's about getting the word out of what you're trying to do. People generally want to help other people. Especially up-and-coming students."

"I can use all the help I can get."

"One of my favorite things about LinkedIn is the ability to search for people in specific industries and specific locations. This allows you to pinpoint industry professionals who might be the closest to what you're looking for."

"Wait, what? You want me to reach out to people I don't even know?"

"People you don't know...yet." C.J. cocked her head and smiled. "You have to remember, these people were once like you, just trying to figure out their next move and build their own network. They know how you feel and where you're coming from. They usually welcome the chance to help out a student, especially someone looking to get into their industry. Of course, you will come across some who don't, but do you really want to be connected to them anyway?"

"Nope, I guess not."

"I'm going to let you in on a secret," C.J. said, leaning forward. "A way to go about this that will increase your chances of making a connection and lead to something more meaningful."

"I'm all ears," said Rory, leaning forward into the conversation himself.

"I see it done wrong all the time," said C.J., shaking her head. "People find someone they don't know on LinkedIn. They just click the Connect button, sending that person a request with absolutely no context and no reason they should connect. Not even a note from the requestor stating their intent. Would you accept that request?"

"Uh, probably not if I didn't know them."

"Exactly. It's crazy how many people send these blind requests to connect and just expect people to accept."

"But I guess I blindly accept new followers on Instagram." Rory said.

"That's different. I assume you just want more followers to make you look like a big deal?"

"Ha, busted!"

"It's okay, I get it. On TikTok, and Instagram, there's clout that comes from having a lot of followers. It's almost an incentive to accept anyone. With business networks like LinkedIn, it's a little different. People usually assume a blind connection is a sales person trying to get their attention so they can sell them something. Truth is, that's usually the case. This makes people skeptical."

"For sure."

"When using LinkedIn on your computer, you can click the Connect button and a box will pop up asking if you want to customize your invitation. Click Add a Note and this will give you the chance to write your personalized message. On LinkedIn's mobile phone app, you have to click the More button and it gives you the option to Personalize Invite."

"Ok, got it," Rory added it to his notes.

"You don't have a lot of characters for your message, so be short and to the point. Mention who you are and why you were hoping to connect. Let them know you're trying to build your network of professionals in the field you're excited about getting into. Do your best to explain yourself so that people understand where you're coming from, that your request is genuine and you're not just trying to sell them something. Like I said, people usually want to help people given the chance."

"Understood."

"Don't make the mistake of reaching out to these professionals and asking for an internship right away. An internship is a bigger commitment, anywhere from two weeks to six months, and it's not very likely that someone who doesn't know you is going to blindly agree to something like that."

"So what do I ask for?"

"Here's another secret," C.J. said. "The first thing you should ask for is an informational interview. This is the chance to ask this person about their own educational journey, their industry, their company and any insights they might have for someone in your situation. This can be done in person, video chat or simply over the phone. Not only are you collecting information to help you better understand if this is the type of industry and job you want to be in, it also allows you to build your network of people who might be able to help you in the future. It doesn't have to be a one-and-done interaction. Maybe you create a friendship and this person could help you find a job shadow, internship or even a real job sometime in the future. That's what building your network is all about. Does that make sense?"

"Yes it does," Rory said. "Problem is, I'm not super comfortable with the thought of having to reach out to these types of people. But at least now I understand how important it is to build my network, and how to use your techniques to be more effective."

"Good. There is another approach I want you to try," C.J. said. "Most universities have alumni programs that connect current students to former students in their desired industry or job type. They usually have an online database of alumni that have agreed to be a part of the program. The school helps match you up so you can connect and ask questions."

"I know, I know… it will help me build my network," Rory said with a smile.

"Exactly. Sounds like it's starting to sink in. I think Payton University's program is called Wildcats@Work. You should definitely check it out."

"I will."

"Okay, Rory, we're just about wrapped up here. I want to thank you again for showing up early and prepared today, and I'm a big fan of your new professional look."

"Thanks," Rory said. "That makes me happy."

"Good enough. Now how about a little homework for the next time we meet up?"

"I'll be honest, I feel pretty overwhelmed," Rory said. "But I trust you and if you say jump, I'll say how high. I know it's what I need."

"Take a little time and create your LinkedIn profile." C.J. said. "It shouldn't take too long. Add all the pertinent information you can think of. Put yourself in a future employer's shoes as you read it and reread it. Make sure there aren't any misspellings. The truth is, you don't have a lot to put on there now, but you'll be doing internships in the future to build up your experience. For now, simply demonstrate that you are open to learning and growing. We can review your profile together when we meet again in a couple of weeks."

"Time to get my act together," Rory said.

"You'll do way better than that. I can't wait to read your new LinkedIn profile. And while you're at it, search LinkedIn's website for more resources for students. They have lots of useful information on networking, communicating on their platform and building your personal brand."

"I'll be sure to do that."

"Oh, and one more thing." C.J. paused, giving extra importance to her next words. "You need to start thinking about your major."

Rory could feel the tension rise in his shoulders and neck. Just the thought of possibly changing majors made him stressed.

"I can see that makes you a little uncomfortable," C.J. said.

"It sure does. Yeah, I mean, I've already started taking civil engineering classes. I'd hate to think I wasted a bunch of money, energy and time on it."

"I totally understand that feeling. But think about how it would feel if you finished that civil engineering degree and went into a career that you don't like at all. That's when people really feel trapped and end up doing it for years. Unhappy and unfulfilled."

"I know you're right," Rory said. "I just need to face it. Time to figure out another option that can support the job I really want in basketball."

"Absolutely. Let me make a suggestion," C.J. said. "Look at all the classes you've taken to this point and see how many of them line up with required classes for a few other majors that might be more in line with what you're passionate about. A lot of your general education requirements like English, math and history are requirements for other majors as well."

"That makes sense." Rory said. "I'll look into it this week. And thanks again for all the great information today. I'm excited to dive into the basketball industry and see what's out there. Wow, a job in basketball. Wouldn't that be something."

"I'm very proud of you, Rory," C.J. said.

Those words rang in his ears all the way back to campus.

Steps to Take

- Start mapping out the types of people who can help you start building your network. Identify the people in your life who might have connections in the industry you're interested in. Likely, you'll just have to start asking people and see where it leads.

- If you haven't already, start exploring Linkedin.com and create your account by filling out all the pertinent information.

/ eleven /

It's Not Losing, Just Learning

"Good morning, Rory," said C.J.'s assistant on the way in. "I like your tie. You dressed up again."

Her assistant's name was Reilly. Great energy and a killer grin. Her warm, soothing voice on the phone when he booked his appointments was something he looked forward to every time.

"Thank you, Reilly."

Just saying her name made his mouth a little dry. He couldn't think of anything else to add, so there was a long awkward pause between them.

"Well, C.J. is ready for you in her office."

"Okay, thanks again." He walked away, distracted, smiling a little.

"Rory! Great to see you," C.J. said. "Looking sharp!"

Her attitude was always contagious. That must be what it felt like to be happy at work.

"Hi C.J.! It's nice to see you too. How are all your businesses going?"

"I won't lie, things have been crazy here, but I do love it. It's great working with people who are passionate about their work and want the team to succeed. Those are things we actually look for in new employees. I've learned over the years that humility in people is one of the most important character traits. It's a cornerstone to great teamwork."

"Humility, huh?" Rory said. "So how do you gauge that in an interview?"

"I've found you have to listen for it. It comes out in the way people talk. When they explain the work they've done, do they use 'we' and 'us' or do they use 'I' and 'me'? Of course, in an interview, you have to talk about yourself, but where you give credit for the work you've accomplished is telling. Are you the hero, or is your entire team?"

"Wow, yeah," Rory said. "I used to have this quote on my gym locker from Kareem Abdul-Jabbar, the 19-time NBA all-star player: *Great players are willing to give up their own personal achievement for the achievement of the group. It enhances everybody.*"

"That's profound."

"When I played, I definitely saw it on the court," Rory said. "There was something amazing about what could be accomplished when everyone came together as a team."

"Absolutely. You can also tell about humility by listening to how people talk about their past bosses or co-workers. If everything is negative and never their fault, likely this kind of attitude will show up when they work for you. I've had people sitting across from me in an interview who I knew could do the job, but I didn't hire them. They had a negative attitude about past managers or coworkers, and it worried me that they might feel this way working with us and not take responsibility for their own actions or fight to make the whole team better."

"That's fascinating. And I can tell you it will make me think twice about my own choice of words in interviews," Rory said.

"I'm going to be extra careful so I don't come across the wrong way."

"Good call," C.J. said. "So how'd it go putting your LinkedIn profile together?"

"Hit and miss. I didn't have a lot of experiences from my past to put on there."

"That's okay. It's good that you're authentic about the experience you *do* have. You don't want to overstate what you've done, and you definitely do not want to lie. Just honestly describe the work you have done. Not having all the experiences you'd like is hopefully motivating to get some internships/apprenticeships and summer jobs that align a little more with where you want to go so you can put them on your resume at some point."

"Sounds good. I've already started thinking about jobs in basketball I might be able to do this summer so I could get more experience and show it on my LinkedIn profile and resume."

"May I see your profile?" C.J. asked.

Rory pulled out his phone, opened the LinkedIn app, clicked on his profile and handed it over to C.J. She scrolled through the information he had added.

"I think this looks great. Nice job."

Rory felt the glow of positive feedback, especially from someone as accomplished as her.

"Can I make a couple of small suggestions?" she asked.

"Uh, sure."

"It's best to have a profile photo that looks a little more professional. I suggest one with just you in the picture. It's also great if it's a little more close up so you can see your face. I'm not saying you need a professional headshot, but maybe have a friend take a picture of you from the shoulders up in better lighting."

The picture Rory had chosen was him with a group of friends. He really liked the shirt he was wearing and his hair looked particularly good that day. He had mostly cropped the others out of the photo, but you could still tell he was standing with a group of people.

"Yeah, no problem. It won't take me long to take a better photo."

"Great, and one more thing. It's tempting for students in your situation who don't have a lot of experience to add to their LinkedIn profile or resume all the little things they did in high school. You put down the French club and some babysitting you did. Unless you're particularly interested in an international internship or something in childhood development, these things are probably not as relevant. It's okay to put the summer jobs you've had, like your landscaping, because it shows something you were committed to for a longer period of time, but likely, as you gain more experience, those things will drop off the list. Do I remember you saying something about being a coach at a kids' basketball camp?"

"That was for a week in the summer between my junior and senior year in high school," Rory said.

"It's worth putting it on there, even though it was a week, because it shows you were interested in experiences particular to the basketball industry."

"That makes sense."

"Okay, once you've made those updates, it's going to be time to reach out to people in the industry. I already explained the importance of including a personal message with each connection request you send. I can't stress the importance of this enough. It will really increase your chances of getting a response."

"I'll make sure to do that."

"All right, once you make those changes to your profile, it's time to start identifying people in the industry that you'd like to be connected to. I was thinking we'd talk a little bit about the specific progression of reaching out and maybe what you could shoot for in terms of a commitment from them. Truth be told, there are all sorts of career learning opportunities out there. Certainly some of the most well-known are career fairs that your school might offer."

"I went to a career fair in high school. Along with some other kids, I took a bus to the city convention center. There were a bunch of companies there with people standing around tables. Students could walk up and ask questions."

"What did you learn?"

"That's the bummer. My friends and I did more goofing around than talking to any of the companies. If I get the chance again, I'm determined to pay a little more attention."

"Career fairs are a decent way to network with people who work at those companies. But the problem is what you will learn and who you will meet is limited to the companies that decided to come to the event. Representatives from companies in the industry you're passionate about might not be there. You could say this is a little more of a passive or reactive approach to making the right industry connections."

"So should I skip going to career fairs?"

"No, I definitely think you should still go. For two reasons. One, you never know who might be there and it just might give you the opportunity to talk to someone in your industry if they're there; and two, it still gives you a chance to see what else is out there. Who knows, maybe a surprise company will peak your interest, or a conversation with someone will inspire you to dig a little deeper about that industry. Remember, no such thing as losing, just learning."

C.J. flashed that smile she always did when she emphasized one of her own quotes.

"Ok, I get it."

"There are three other opportunities we should talk a little more about. These three require you to be more proactive, but can really help you gain more information about the industry you are passionate about and build your network. They are informational interviews, job shadows and internships."

"Right, I know we talked about those."

"Yes. Remember, identifying and connecting with people in the industry and understanding the career learning opportunities you'd like to get are all part of the Design phase. Setting up conversations with those people and actually going and doing those opportunities is the Exploration phase."

"Okay, got it."

"So let's start with informational interviews. Like I've said, lots of professionals out there are willing to help out a student. They remember a time in their life when they weren't completely sure how they were going to navigate their own future and the thought of having someone to guide them is really appealing. Many want to offer that helping hand."

"But don't they think I'm just bugging them? I don't want to be a nuisance or an interruption."

"Yes, some do, but not most. People want to find a way to give back. They want to help someone else, but they don't always get that opportunity. This is a chance for them to be able to offer some guidance and it's really not a big imposition or time commitment for them. Don't you want to be in a position some day to help a student like you?"

"Absolutely," Rory said.

"Exactly. So let's talk about how you go about it. First, you have to identify who you want to talk to. Of course, this takes some time, but think of it as building your network.

Remember, I said your network can be a really valuable thing in the future when you're looking for bigger things like internships and an actual job. Relationships you've built with people who can possibly help you. Or even you helping them someday."

"You've always talked about investing in myself," Rory said.

"That's it! You've already started reaching out to the people closest to you. Now start doing some web searches about basketball in the city and see what you come up with. Coaches, companies and so on. Start making a list of potential leads. You might have to dig deep. If you find a company that's involved with basketball, you might have to call their office and ask around. Is there someone there who you can ask some questions about the industry? I guarantee you aren't the first student to call asking these types of questions."

"I have to tell you, just having to call someone out of the blue gives me the cold sweats," Rory said. "I'll just feel like a nuisance."

"Understandable. But the first call is the hardest. It always gets easier from there."

"I believe you."

"Don't forget to ask your professors who they might know. Or even call the athletic department at Payton. They have lots of connections. Whether you use LinkedIn, direct messaging on another social media platform or just outright email or call someone, be sure to give them context. It can be really simple. Something like this."

C.J. tilted back in her chair and looked at the ceiling as she spoke.

"Hi, my name is Rory Langford and I'm a student at Payton University. I'm really interested in the field of basketball as a career and I'm trying to learn more about jobs in the industry. I was

wondering if you had 15-20 minutes where I might be able to ask you a few questions. We could do it over the phone, video chat or I could meet you at your office. I'm sure you're incredibly busy, so thank you so much for considering this. Thanks again, Rory Langford."

"It's perfect. Can you write all my introductions?"

They laughed together.

"That's the formula," C.J. said. "Introduction, specific request and thank you. Take it and run with it. And at the end of your note, don't forget to give your contact information."

"For sure," Rory said.

"And when you schedule a meeting, make it as easy as possible for the person you're reaching out to. That might mean getting up early to meet them before work, or going after work, at lunch or whatever is convenient for them. Be flexible."

"Again, great advice."

"And because you don't know much about this person, it's always safest to meet in a public place. If it's not at their office during normal business hours, someplace like a popular coffee shop is a good bet, but a video chat can be just as useful."

"Understood."

"Once you've scheduled a meeting or a call, you'll need to come up with some questions you'll want to ask." She turned and typed on her computer.

"I'm emailing you some questions I like. Let me know when you get them."

Rory's phone pinged, and he read out loud:

"What did your career path look like? What are the best parts of your job? The worst? Other than *your* job, what other interesting jobs do you see in the industry? How do you see this industry changing? What jobs are needed in the future? What advice do you have for someone like me trying to get into the industry? Could I possibly contact you again with any questions that might come up later?"

"Those are good ones, and you may have more," C.J. said. "When you meet, I highly recommend you bring a notebook and a pen to take some notes. Start a fresh notebook specifically for this type of thing. Keep all your thoughts in one place. If you do forget or decide to keep notes on your phone, make sure you tell them that is what you're doing. The last thing you want them to think is that you're on your phone texting or doing something else. It could give off the feeling that they're not important to you. You certainly don't want them to think you're wasting their time."

Rory thought about all the times he'd been on his phone in front of other people, even C.J. Was he giving off the wrong message? He'd have to work a little harder on that one.

"You look lost in thought all of a sudden," C.J. said.

"No. Sorry. Yeah, I definitely wouldn't want them to get that impression. I appreciate anyone that takes the time to help me out."

"That's good, because you're probably not going to like my next suggestion. But it's surprisingly effective."

"Ok, what is it?"

"It's important to send a handwritten thank-you card as a follow up."

"I was afraid of that," Rory said. "Mom always asked me to do that after relatives sent birthday and holiday gifts. I'll admit, I'm not very good at it. I really didn't follow up that often, if at all."

"That's the genius of it," C.J. countered. "In today's world, nobody does, so you'll stand out. It means a lot to the person who receives it because the gesture is so rare. People appreciate the extra effort you put in and that shines on you. Maybe you'll want to reach out to that person in the future because you want to ask about internships/apprenticeships or you see a job at their company. They will be more likely to remember you and the card."

For a moment, Rory wondered if he could send belated thank-you cards to his grandparents for all the gifts over the years. *Never too late to be thankful, right?*

"Really, this is true whenever you get the chance to meet with someone who is helping you or has influence over a decision about you, like a job interview. Sending handwritten thank-you notes right after the meeting always helps you stand out."

"That's a good one, C.J. I really appreciate the tip, and I'll do my best. So, how many informational interviews should I try to get?"

"I'm not sure you can really ever do *too many*. You can learn so much from each one. The more you do, the more people you meet and the bigger your network grows. The more you put into it, the more you'll get out of it. My minimum suggestion is doing at least four or five. It should be no later than during your sophomore and junior year at college. And of course, the earlier you do it, like your freshman year, the more informed you are about what kind of classes and degree work best if you want to pursue a job in that industry. But the great thing is, it's never too late. Even if you want to switch industries someday, informational interviews can still be valuable for learning and growing your network. "

"In some ways, I wish I had started earlier," Rory said. "Although, as you say, it's a winding path. I guess now's the time to get going."

"You're well on your way," C.J. said in a warm and encouraging tone. "Now you've got some work to do over the next few weeks. Start identifying some people you'd like to contact for informational interviews and begin reaching out. When we get back together you can tell me how it went."

"I have no idea what I'm doing," Rory said. "But nothing to lose, right?"

"Yes indeed," C.J. said. "And everything to gain. You've got this."

On his way out of the building, Rory craned his head everywhere hoping to see Reilly, but she was nowhere to be found.

Steps to Take

- Start doing research on companies and people in your industry. Check job posting websites for examples of different job types. Read job descriptions. Find out who you'd like to talk to.

- Write a short, direct pitch letter to introduce yourself and state your purpose.

- Approach those people using the tools mentioned above and your letter.

- Create a list of questions you would like to use in an informational interview.

- Schedule your first informational interview.

/ twelve /

Putting in the Work

"Hey, what's that?"

"I got us a pizza," Xavier said. "You've barely gotten up from that laptop all day. Time for a well-deserved break."

"Ok, sold," Rory said and shut his laptop. "Smells incredible."

Xavier pushed aside the notebooks and computer and made the desk into a table.

"Mmmmm, so good. Thanks, man," Rory said.

"Least I can do. You've been hard at it."

"So have you," Rory said. "You've been spending a lot of time down at the university career center."

"Just trying to keep up with you. What are you working on now?"

Rory told him about his research, about the informational interviews and the introduction notes he was trying to get right, as the boys devoured the sausage and pepperoni pizza.

"Look at us, getting all serious about our careers," Xavier said. "When we met it was all sports and video games."

Rory laughed. "You're right. So what's happening at the career center?"

"It's way better than I imagined," Xavier said. "They actually have a lot of connections with businesses who are interested in talking with students. Last slice of pizza. That's yours."

"Nope, that's yours," Rory said. "I need to get down to the center myself."

"I'll show you around anytime," Xavier said.

"Have you narrowed down your industry yet?"

"Actually, I have. I think I want to learn more about the entertainment industry, particularly music."

"That doesn't surprise me at all. You're always talking about music and it's clear it's one of your passions."

"Yeah, thanks," Xavier said. "I guess, kind of like basketball for you, it always felt a little unrealistic. I never let myself dream of a career making money in music. But I've been doing a lot of research online, and I've been looking into sound engineering and producing. I think working in a recording studio would be awesome."

"You'd be so good at that," Rory said. "I can already see you sitting behind the mixing board directing the artists."

Xavier laughed. "Thanks man, I'm excited to explore it a bit more. I'm also interested in learning what it takes to be the one who puts on a performing arts show. You know, like those singing contests on TV or even a football halftime show. I don't even know yet what that job is, but it seems cool."

"All right, when you're a bigshot in Los Angeles or New York, don't forget about us little people. At least get me some free tickets."

"No problemo."

"Thanks for the pizza. Now I'm going to keep pestering basketball people."

Rory turned back to his computer. What he wanted to do was try to search for Reilly and find out more about her. At this point he didn't even know her last name. But in his newfound spirit of productivity, he resisted that urge. Instead, taking C.J.'s suggestion, decided to see if anyone on the Payton University basketball staff could offer him some advice. He went to the Payton University website and looked up the names of the coaching staff. There he saw the head coach, two assistant coaches, a strength and conditioning coach, a dietician, a video and analytics coordinator and director of basketball operations. He was surprised to see their email addresses also listed next to their names.

The director of basketball operations was a woman named Jenny Chen. Her bio said she'd been with the program for more than 13 years in different capacities. She'd been the assistant director of basketball operations, director of video operations, graduate assistant and student manager. Rory was impressed. He guessed she had put in her time in an effort to work her way up. It looked like her hard work and dedication were paying off. He decided she was the right person for him to talk to, and he took his time to write her an email:

Dear Ms. Chen,

My name is Rory and I'm a student here at Payton University. It's impressive to see how you've worked hard and grown with the Payton basketball program. I'm at a bit of a crossroads trying to learn more about what I want to pursue in the professional world. I'm really passionate about basketball and interested in learning about job opportunities in the field.

I was wondering if you might consider a 20-minute informational meeting with me where I can ask some questions and learn from your successes?

I would appreciate your consideration. Thank you so much,

Rory Langford
rory.langford@payton.edu
555-555-4971

Now he had to wait to see what he got back. In the meantime, he thought he'd put some more of C.J.'s advice to work and reach out to a few people via LinkedIn. He'd found two companies of particular interest and thought it'd be worthwhile to send messages to their human resources department.

He knew HR dealt with employee administration in hiring, firing, payroll and insurance, and figured they could at least lead him in the right direction.

One of the companies he'd found was called Excel Sports Camps. They offered week-long camps to kids ages eight to fourteen. These camps helped kids learn the fundamentals of all types of sports and be evaluated on their performance to better understand what they could work on. Rory had heard about the company when he was younger, but had never taken a camp himself.

The other company was a new basketball shoe company called Elevate. Rory had seen their ads in Sports Illustrated magazine and their style was cool. This interested him greatly, since he'd always liked the fashion side of sports, especially shoes. He liked the idea of combining two passions, basketball and fashion, to see what that would be like.

After a little searching, he found the general information email address for Excel Sports Camps. It was not exactly what he wanted, since he was hoping to find an actual person to reach out to, but figured it was a start. For Elevate, he found a blog post written by the director of marketing, a person named Damien Clark. Rory decided to start with him.

He pulled up LinkedIn and searched for Damien Clark. A number of profiles came up, but he kept scrolling until he found Damien Clark, Director of Marketing, Elevate Footwear. Rory looked over his profile and saw that he had gone to college at New York University and then worked in fashion in New York for a few different clothing companies before coming to Elevate. Rory decided to send him a request to connect by clicking the *Connect* button on Mr. Clark's LinkedIn profile. By doing this, he knew from C.J. he would be able to send a note to personalize his invitation. He then clicked *Add a Note* and typed out his request:

Hello Mr. Clark,

My name is Rory Langford and I'm a student at Payton University. I'm reaching out since I'm doing some career exploration, and I want to learn as much as I can about the basketball industry. I find the combination of basketball and fashion incredibly fascinating.

I saw an article you wrote about how shoe technology is changing to benefit different kinds of players. I was hoping I might be able to ask you a few questions about Elevate and the whole basketball field. Please let me know if you might be up for a 15-minute informational interview.

I don't want to take up too much of your time, but I would be extremely grateful for the chance to learn from you.

I hope you consider my request. Thank you so much!

Rory Langford
rory.langford@payton.edu
555-555-4971

Once Rory was finished, he reread his message two more times to make sure he'd spelled everything correctly and that it all made sense. Then he clicked *Done* to send his request. He wasn't sure what he might get back, if anything, but it was his chance to grow his network with someone in the industry. Who knew where it might lead?

Then Rory remembered he still had to send a note to Excel Sports Camps. Because he only had the general information email for Excel, he knew he had to change his message a little, but could still use some of the same things he'd written for his message to Elevate Footwear. Rory copied and pasted the email address into his Gmail account and started typing:

Hello,

My name is Rory Langford and I'm a student at Payton University. I'm reaching out since I'm doing some career exploration. I want to learn as much as I can about the basketball industry.

I see that you run youth sports camps. I grew up playing basketball myself and love the idea of helping kids become their very best. I was wondering if there was someone within the organization that I might be able to talk to about what it's like to work in sports, and specifically, in the basketball field. I would really welcome the chance.

Thank you so much for considering my request,

Rory Langford
rory.langford@payton.edu
555-555-4971

Again, Rory reread his message twice to make sure there weren't any misspellings and it all flowed together. Once he felt confident it was ready, he clicked *Send* and the email was off. Although Xavier was gone and he was all alone, he stood up and did a fist pump. This felt huge. He had just sent three different requests out into the basketball industry. What would happen next?

Now it was time to reward himself. He put on his favorite jersey and headed out for a pickup game of basketball. He'd been so busy working on his career that he'd been missing the games. He felt stiff from staring at his laptop so long. Some hoops would definitely do him good.

On his way to the gym, he thought about those queries he'd just sent out. He couldn't believe how good it felt to take action in the direction of his dreams. Would anyone write him back? He couldn't wait to find out.

And… maybe he'd better call Reilly and confirm his next appointment. Any excuse to talk to her. She was the kind of person he hoped he could meet someday when he was successful, when he'd figured all this out and was actually worthy of someone like her. But before he called, he tried to think of something charming and funny to say, a way to make an impression and make her laugh.

Finally he called, but he didn't get Reilly, just her office voicemail. All the same, he could have listened to that voice all day.

Steps to Take

- Once you do the research, find some people to reach out to. Get some practice sending these emails.

- First impressions are important. Make sure to reread your messages to ensure there are no misspellings and they are as professional as possible.

- To increase your chances of making good connections, it's likely you'll have to send out a number of requests. People get busy, forget to respond or doubt themselves that they have much to offer. Keep trying.

/ thirteen /

The Core of the Matter

"New meeting place, huh?"

Rory found C.J. in her office gym, already warming up. It was strange to see her in sweats, as if he'd assumed that she dressed so sharp 24/7.

"Hope this works for you," C.J. said, tossing him a towel and some water. "I've got back-to-back meetings all day, but I wasn't about to miss our conversation. I'm really enjoying watching your progress, Rory. Plus, you make a commitment, you stick with it. Glad to see you dressed for a workout."

She hopped on a high-tech-looking curved treadmill machine and began pacing.

"All yours," she indicated a similar machine beside her.

Rory got on and tried to get a feeling for the thing, walking tentatively at first.

"So, how did it go?" C.J. asked, picking up her speed a little. "I'm dying to know."

"You'll be happy to know I'm two for three," Rory said. "Here, I'll read you what I got back."

He tried to focus on his phone and his walking. He'd seen too many funny videos of people wiping out on treadmills. Meanwhile, C.J. was moving at an impressive pace.

"Ok, here's email number one," Rory said. "From Jenny Chen, Payton University's director of basketball operations."

"Payton University, you reached out," C.J. said. "Nice job."

"Dear Rory," he read. "Thanks so much for reaching out. I love that you're looking into basketball as a potential career opportunity. There are a lot of cool jobs out there for fans like us. Why don't you come down to the athletic center, here on campus, and we can talk more about your efforts. And if I can't answer your questions, maybe I know someone else in my network who can. How about Thursday, the 24th at 3 p.m.? Let me know. Looking forward to meeting you, Jenny. P.S. Go Wildcats!"

"All RIGHT!" C.J. reached out for a high five. Her slap was unexpectedly strong.

"Okay, give me 30 seconds here," she said.

She pressed a button a few times and the machine went into hyperdrive. Her feet flew and arms pumped high as she kept up. A chime sounded and the machine slowed again.

"Intervals," she panted. "Best thing ever to kick start your day."

"Impressive," Rory said. "Here, I'll read you the next one. Not quite as great, but still a response: Hello Mr. Langford. Though we appreciate your interest in Excel Sports Camps, we are a small organization and unfortunately are too busy to meet with you. If you are interested in applying to be a coach with our program, please watch for openings on our website in the spring. We wish you the best of luck, Jamie Riggens, Excel Sports Camps."

"How do you feel about that one?" C.J. said as she ran.

"Disappointed, but you told me it would happen. Not everyone I reached out to would make time to respond, let alone meet with me. At least they emailed me back. I know I'll just have to reach out to more people if I want to keep growing my network."

"One hundred percent," C.J. said. "Especially if you want to make enough contacts to increase your chances for job shadows and internships. Okay, here I go again."

Again her feet were a blur and Rory marveled at her speed and stamina. He turned up his machine and picked up his own pace.

"All right Rory," C.J. said, slowing down again. "You showed heart and discipline to get those replies. Nice work. Though there is more to do, you also need to focus a bit on your major. I know this can all feel like a lot."

"It really does," Rory said, a little winded already from his faster pace.

"For sure. Just remember what I said about the winding path. You're making the effort now to set yourself up for success. All of these decisions are moving you in a direction that is more aligned with who you are as a person. And when you're more aligned with who you are, you will begin to feel more fulfilled. All of these curves on the winding path are typical."

"No losing, just learning, right?" Rory said. "I just want to make sure I'm on the right track."

"Stand by," C.J. said, and went into superwoman speed one more time. There was no way Rory was going to try that.

"Okay," she said, stepping off the treadmill and toweling off. "I totally understand, but, I do want to let you in on a little secret."

Rory shut down his own machine and looked at C.J. intently.

"There is no perfect major," she said. "Of course, there are a few specialty majors that are necessary to go directly into that field of work, but even that doesn't guarantee someone a job, let alone one they're sure to love. Lots of people lock in their degree and then seek out experiences like job shadows and internships in the industry they're passionate about. Ready for some squats?"

"Sure," Rory said. "I'm stressed about changing my major, and I'm back and forth on whether civil engineering is a waste of my time."

"Ok," C.J. said, setting up the squat rack. "Ready for a set?"

"Sure," Rory said. C.J. waited while he went through a few squats. She took the bar next, and went much deeper than he had and knocked out more reps. Once again, impressive. She racked the bar.

"Something I wanted to tell you…" Rory said. "Strange, but there are some parts of my coursework I've really enjoyed. Specifically my industrial engineering classes."

"Really?" C.J. said. "Very interesting. Go on."

"Mom was right, I do like to make things. The process of how a product or machine comes together is really interesting to me. I like how you need the right design, analysis and manufacturing processes to create something. With civil engineering, those are applied to things like roads, bridges, and buildings. I just don't think those things are interesting."

"That makes sense," C.J. said. "But what if you were applying that industrial engineering process to a product in basketball? Like developing a new automatic shot rebounder or a basketball or even apparel like a pair of shoes? That's just it. Taking a skill or an interest that you're good at and applying it to an industry you're passionate about. Your turn."

Rory did a few more squats, his form improving as he went, trying to mirror C.J.'s.

"Funny you mention shoes" Rory said, once she was done with her own set. "I reached out to a guy named Damien Clark on LinkedIn. He's the director of marketing at Elevate Shoes."

"I know Damien." C.J. said. "My recruiting firm has done work for Elevate. He's a really nice guy."

"No way! Are you serious?"

"Have you heard back from him?"

"Unfortunately, not yet."

"Maybe I could reach out to him and put in a good word," she said with a smile.

"Oh wow. That would be amazing."

"No problem, I'll do it later today." C.J. said. "One more set of squats for us both."

He stepped up, shouldered the bar and knocked out some halfway respectable squats this time.

"Rory, look into what it would take to change your major from civil to industrial engineering. You've probably already taken a lot of the necessary classes."

"Ok, but what could I do with an industrial engineering degree in the basketball field? I assumed I'd have to change my major completely."

"If manufacturing interests you then an industrial engineering degree would be a great fit and you could look for companies manufacturing products for the basketball industry. And honestly, you don't have to be the one directly involved in manufacturing for a degree like that to be useful. Do you know what a project manager is?"

"I don't."

"Give me a sec." C.J. did her last set of squats, then racked the bar and began pulling weights off. Rory did the same on his side.

"A project manager is responsible for planning and overseeing projects to ensure they are completed on time and on budget," she said. "Project managers plan and designate project resources, prepare budgets, monitor progress and keep everyone informed along the way. Having an industrial engineering degree and understanding the manufacturing process can really be valuable to a job like that. Hiring managers like engineering degrees because it shows an adherence to a rigorous curriculum. They like to see that you didn't shy away from taking hard classes."

"I can certainly attest to that," said Rory, wincing.

"I've known a number of people who finished engineering degrees and went on to do things in business operations, finance and marketing." C.J. said.

"Honestly, I'd never thought of that. I'll talk to my advisor and learn more about an industrial engineering degree. Thanks for explaining that."

"Happy to. Time for some core work. My favorite part."

"Not mine," said Rory, grabbing a mat and following her.

"So when are you meeting Jenny, director of basketball operations?"

"We're meeting on the 24th. And thanks to you, I have my list of questions ready."

"Nice work." C.J. said. "That's a great connection to make."

"I'm just bummed that the local sports camp company is too busy to meet with me."

"Yeah, that happens. But don't forget it's not just local companies either. If you find one farther away that's really interesting, you could always ask for a phone or video interview. That could still turn out to be a good, informative connection and even come in handy if they have summer internships that you're willing to travel to. A lot of students will take a paid internship in a different city over the summer if it offers the experience they're looking for. This always looks good on a resume too."

"Awesome."

"Well, hopefully we can get Damien to spend a little time with you. I think he could definitely be a good contact and give you a little different perspective since he's on the marketing side of things."

"If anyone can make it happen, it's you."

"This is great progress, Rory. I'm delighted to see you digging in and learning more about your passion industry. I have a feeling these connections are really going to pay off."

"So do I," Rory said. "I'm starting to feel a weight lifted off my shoulders, and not just your squat bar."

"It's great to see you executing the Design phase. I want you to keep reaching out to people even when you start the Exploration phase of meeting with these connections. Those two phases can work in tandem. Next time we meet, I'll be excited to hear what you find out about switching your major over to industrial engineering, if that's really what you want to do, and hearing how these meetings go. And now, it is time for a few minutes of my favorite core workout. You're not going to like me very much."

She was right.

fourteen

A Call Out of the Blue

"Hey Mom, it's your long-lost son," Rory said into his phone.

"So happy to hear from you, Rory. I assumed you lost my number since I haven't heard from you in so long."

"Very funny, Mom. I just wanted to tell you my latest thoughts."

"I'd love to hear them, son."

"I talked to my advisor at the university, and it turns out I've already taken a lot of the core classes necessary to get an industrial engineering degree."

"That's great news," his mom said.

"And, after thinking it over, I'm also leaning towards the marketing side of basketball. Being able to work with a company and help sell or promote their products seems really interesting. I want others to get as excited about basketball as I am."

"From what I know of you, it seems like a dream job."

"Yes, and you know how you always pointed out my love of making things? You were right, I want to use that in some way. Getting an industrial engineering degree would help me do that, even if I didn't end up working in manufacturing."

"If anything, it sounds like it gives you options."

"Exactly! And I'm wondering about getting a marketing or communications minor. Seems like this combination would make me more marketable to companies, and would show my process oriented skills along with creative thinking skills."

"You're really taking this seriously," his mom said. "C.J. must be rubbing off on you."

"Yes I am, and she's been amazing," Rory said. "Just to be sure, I've done a lot of research on industrial engineering. I read articles online and watched a lot of videos on YouTube to make sure this aligned with my expectations. By now I have a pretty good idea what an actual day in the life of an industrial engineer looks like."

"Well, you've done your due diligence. You certainly have my blessing."

"Okay, Mom," Rory swallowed hard. "That does it. Thanks for the vote of confidence. I'm going down and officially switching my major to industrial engineering. It's all starting to feel like I'm aligning with who I really am and want to be."

"Well, listen to my boy. I'm proud of you," his mom said. "I love you, Rory. I know you'll do great. Bye, son."

"Bye, mom."

He had just ended the call when a strange number flashed on his phone. Telemarketer. Normally he'd ignore the call, but this time he decided to roll the dice.

"Hello?"

"I'm calling for Rory."

"That's me." Definitely a telemarketer. He pulled the phone away to hang up.

"Rory, what's up? This is Damien Clark from Elevate Footwear. How's it going?"

He stared at his phone in disbelief.

"Oh, hey, Mr. Clark, it's really great to hear from you." His voice sounded high and squeaky.

"Whoa, call me Damien. We're pretty chill around here."

"Okay, cool. Well thanks Mr. Clark. I mean Damien. Sorry, I'll get it right."

"It's all good. You must be doing something right to have C.J. Parker in your corner. She says some pretty great things about you."

It's not what you know, but who you know. Rory smiled. *Thanks, Mr. Thomas, and thanks, C.J.*

"Thanks so much, Damien. C.J. is great. She's been an awesome mentor for me. I've been working hard trying to figure out what I want to do with school and honestly, the rest of my life, and she's been really helpful in working through it with me."

"Yes, she's one saavy business person. Elevate has been really lucky to have her working on our recruiting."

How did she fit it all in? Rory appreciated the time they'd spent together even more.

"Anyway, she told me I was crazy if I at least didn't make time to catch up with you. And I always listen to C.J.. I gotta be honest, right now I'm really, really busy, because we're launching a new signature shoe in a couple of weeks with a big up-and-coming NBA rookie. But I was wondering if we could do a video conference over the computer. Would that be all right?"

"Yes, absolutely," said Rory, trying to keep his voice from trembling.

"Well, I'm excited to meet you Rory. How about this Friday after lunch. Say 1:30 p.m.?"

"My classes get done at noon on Friday, so that's perfect. I'm really looking forward to it."

"Right on. C.J. gave me your email so I'll shoot you over a meeting invite with a link for a video chat. We'll see you then. Thanks, Rory."

"Thank *you,* Damien!"

The call ended and Rory sat for a moment in disbelief. He couldn't believe he'd just been on the phone with the director of marketing for Elevate Footwear and soon they'd be having an informational interview video chat. So cool. All of a sudden, the work was paying off. His life was taking some very interesting turns.

fifteen

Go, Wildcats!

Rory showed up to the athletic center fifteen minutes before his meeting with Ms. Chen. He wanted to make sure he was there on time. He knew that punctuality was a sign of respect to the person you are meeting, and after how he'd felt showing up late that time to see C.J., he wasn't about to repeat his mistake.

A sign in the lobby said, Administrative Offices, third floor. Rory decided to take the stairs. After his relatively weak showing on C.J.'s treadmill, a little exercise would probably do him good. On the third floor was a reception desk with a young man about his age behind it. Probably a student on work study.

"Welcome to the University Athletic Center. I'm Gabe. Who are you here to see, please?"

"I have a 3 p.m. with Ms. Chen," Rory said.

"Great, why don't you have a seat and I'll let Jenny know you're here."

Rory thanked him and sat down on one of the purple couches. School colors, of course. On the walls were plaques and memorabilia for conference titles from many of the different Payton sports teams. Rory loved seeing all the history. *What a cool place to work.*

A tall, athletic-looking woman approached.

"You must be Rory. I'm Jenny."

"Yes, thanks so much for taking the time to meet with me. I've got all sorts of questions for you."

"Great," she said. "I'm happy to help. Why don't we head back to my office."

Rory followed Jenny as they headed down the hall. Jenny's office had even more Payton basketball memorabilia all over her shelves and desk. Almost every square inch was covered. She was even wearing purple.

"You certainly have a lot of school spirit," he said.

"What do you think, too much?"

"No, I think it's great," Rory said. "I saw that you've actually worked for this basketball program for quite a while."

"Yes, it's been thirteen years. I started out as the manager of the women's basketball team. I actually went to school at Payton and though I didn't get recruited, I was hoping to walk on and play here. Unfortunately, it didn't really work out that way, but I still really wanted to be a part of the team. My senior year they had an opening for the team manager. I applied, and now here I am."

"I think that's awesome." Rory said. "Is it okay if I ask a few questions?"

"Fire away," she said. "I'm ready."

"Okay, thanks. When you applied for the manager position, was it your plan to be in basketball when you finished school and try to move up the ranks with the team?"

"No not really," Jenny said. "At the time, I was getting an accounting degree and figured I would probably go work for a big corporation somewhere or one of the big accounting firms. But ultimately, I really liked being a part of the Payton team.

Once I graduated, I decided to go back and get my masters in business administration. While going to school, I was a graduate assistant helping both the men's and women's team doing video work. It was a paid position, so it was a way to help pay for school, get some more experience and still be a part of the team."

"That seems smart." Rory said.

"Yes, I guess it turned out to be," she said. "If you can get paid while you get some experience then it's always valuable. I guess I'd already proven myself a bit as the team manager. That was *all* volunteer, and plenty of hours at that."

"I bet," Rory said.

"When I really asked myself what I wanted to do, I realized I was right where I should be. I loved working for Payton, I loved the basketball teams and wanted to further my career in this industry."

"Did you ever have any other things you wanted to do? Do you ever miss accounting?"

"Yeah, I guess a little. I've always wondered what that might have looked like, but I was having a really good time in an industry that I loved. It was hard to beat."

"What about working for another team?" Rory asked.

"Another good question. I thought about it, but I guess they liked my work. I kept getting offered new opportunities to grow my skills and responsibilities here. And now I'm the director of basketball operations over both programs. I love my job."

"That's very cool. I appreciate you sharing your journey with me. Are you okay with a few more questions?"

"Absolutely."

"What are the best parts of your job? And I know it's probably not perfect everyday, so what are the worst parts?"

"I have to tell the worst parts, too? Wow, you want to know all the dirt." Jenny smiled, folded her arms and sat back in her chair.

"Well, I guess the best parts would be coordinating all the needs the coaches have to make sure our student athletes get the very best experience. It's fun to know my efforts help make our programs run smoothly overall and I know our fans appreciate that, too."

"And does it always run smoothly?"

"Ha, well, not all the time. And maybe that's the worst part. To ensure it does go as smoothly as possible, I work a lot of long hours. But I really love the work and this place. We have a good team culture and appreciative staff, and that makes it all worth it."

Rory had heard about the importance of culture. He thought back to C.J.'s office and how her employees interacted, respected and appreciated each other.

"Okay, you know I'm looking at my future, and I love the sport of basketball," Rory said. "So what other cool jobs do you see in the basketball industry?"

"You know, there are a lot, actually, more than you'd think. Our programs have all sorts of different positions that help make this place run, from trainers to strength and conditioning coaches to travel administrators and video operations like I did. Not to mention all the administrative jobs in our general university athletic department including marketing, social media, facilities management, accounting, finance and lots of others."

Rory glanced down at his notebook. "What advice do you have for someone like me who is interested in getting a job in the industry?"

"Sure, but first, why don't you tell me a little bit about you and what you're hoping to accomplish? I want to make sure I'm giving you the very best direction I can."

"I really appreciate that," Rory said. "And I appreciate your time today. I'd say I'm kind of like you. I've always loved basketball. Walking on to play basketball in college would have been a dream, but it wasn't in my cards either. Honestly, I gave up on basketball. I never thought of it as an actual job. I always thought you had to be the one going pro to really ever make a living out of it. I didn't ever think about all the other jobs in the industry that I could do that played into my love of the sport."

"That's fairly typical," Jenny said. "Most students think exactly the way you did."

"But then I met this businesswoman, C.J., who made me stop and think what I was really passionate about. She made me take some time to be introspective and dream big about what I wanted to be spending my time doing in my professional career, then understand the industries around that passion. Knowing that if I would live true to my unique interests and passions, I'd be more fulfilled in life. C.J. says, 'Be more like you.'"

"Wow, you're lucky to have had someone to challenge you. I know a lot of students who are equally unsure about what they want to do, but they don't approach it nearly as well. And they definitely don't give it enough time and energy to truly get aligned like you have."

"I was actually going for a civil engineering degree, but honestly, it's just not what I'm passionate about. I think engineering is cool, but I'm more interested in the process of manufacturing and how things come together. I want to integrate this with my true passion for basketball. So I think

I'm going to change to industrial engineering and possibly look at project management or product marketing."

"It sounds like a good plan."

"So I would really appreciate any advice you'd have for someone like me," Rory said.

"I think you're going down the right path, Rory. Meeting with people like me in the industry is really important, as well as getting to see the day-to-day activities of the job you want. You have to build that network of people who know you and ultimately could be a good resource for possible job shadows, internships/apprenticeships and career opportunities. And actually, I have someone who I think you should meet. There is a new innovative company that we've been working with for our training. Their name is DribbleSync. They make a smart basketball that improves ball handling skills through gamification and real-time feedback. The ball has embedded accelerometers to track the ball's movement and send the information to an app on your phone. Their target market is more of the newer, up-and-coming basketball players, but our teams have been testing it with them and they actually like the drills training."

"Wow, yeah, Jenny, I'd love to meet anyone at that company. It sounds pretty cool."

"Kari Williams is the director of product marketing over there. I can give her a call and see if she'll meet with you. You never know, maybe she has internships or something like that available."

"That would be really great. Thank you so much, Jenny."

"Of course Rory. It's been a pleasure to get to know you. If there is ever anything I can do for you please don't hesitate to ask. I know what it feels like to need help from another to catch a break in this industry. We have to help each other out."

"That means the world to me, Jenny. I'll certainly let you know."

He shook Jenny's hand and thanked her for her time. On his walk back to his dorm, Rory thought about the web of people he was starting to weave together. It started with C.J., but now it included Jenny and soon he'd be able to meet Damien at Elevate. He felt a happy buzz from seeing his efforts pay off and gratitude for all the help along the way.

With C.J.'s voice ringing in his ears, he sat right down and wrote a thank-you note to Jenny.

/ sixteen /

Show Me Your Hustle

Rory sat down in front of his laptop and blew out a big breath. Just about time for his video chat with Damien, and he was feeling the pressure.

Next to his laptop in front of him was a notebook with all his questions carefully written down. He'd rehearsed the call in his head and practiced the questions several times. He'd also checked the link Damien had sent and downloaded the right video conferencing software to make sure he didn't have any glitches. He didn't want any surprises, and he definitely wanted to make a good impression.

He had also done some research on Elevate so he would have some specific items to talk about and show Damien that he *was* truly interested in the company.

Ok, 1:30 p.m. Go time.

Rory clicked the link, and his computer's camera and microphone kicked in. Damien was already there waiting. He was clean cut and friendly looking and stylishly dressed.

"Hey Rory, what's up?" Damien said with a smile.

"Not much, Damien. I hope I'm not late."

"You're right on time."

"Awesome. Well, I can't thank you enough for meeting with me. Thanks for setting up this video call."

"Absolutely." Damien said. "We use them all the time."

Rory knew from his research that Elevate sponsored Jason Altman.

"So I've gotta ask, Damien. Do you think Altman and The Lakers have a chance of sweeping the Timberwolves in the finals? Everyone is talking about how his game keeps getting better in clutch situations, and his stats sure are climbing right now."

On the screen, Damien cracked a huge smile.

"Pretty amazing right? That guy is really having a great season. Yeah, I think there is a chance they could beat Minnesota. A sweep would be tough, but you never know. So tell me about you. What's your story?"

"Well, I'm kind of on a new journey," Rory said. "I thought I was interested in civil engineering, but I wasn't really loving those classes. I had to really ask myself if that's what I really wanted to do with the rest of my life."

"Hey, I understand where you're coming from," Damien said. "Believe it or not, I initially thought I was interested in architecture. I loved to draw, but to make any money, I thought you had to do something more professional."

Damien made air quotes when he said the word "professional" and rolled his eyes. Rory laughed.

"Isn't it funny?" Damien said. "How we worry about what other people think of our choices instead of really leaning in to what *we* want for ourselves."

"Man, I totally agree."

"Well, at least you did figure it out," Damien said.

"I'm still working on it." Rory said. "That's why I'm glad I get to talk to you."

"Of course, how can I help?"

The first question that came to Rory's mind wasn't even on his list.

"I know you're a busy guy. Why would you even meet with me in the first place? There's nothing in it for you."

"Ha!" Damien sat back and laughed. "That's a great question. I appreciate you asking."

Rory could see Damien looking around as he collected his thoughts.

"I guess I know what it feels like to be in your place. Just trying to get some advice to figure your next steps. Trying to meet some people. I know there are plenty of people who wouldn't return your phone call or emails, because they think they have too much going on. I've been there. But really, there are a ton of people who recognize the importance of helping out someone who is just trying to find their way. Generally, I think most people in the professional world want to do whatever they can to help. Yes, it probably won't benefit them directly, but you never know."

"Good to know."

Damien shifted in his chair. "Actually, I met with a student about five years ago. She was just finishing up her marketing degree and we did an informational interview like this. She ended up going on to work at a big energy drink company based in Los Angeles. We stayed in touch here and there and about a year ago I reached out to her and through that contact, she hooked me up with their VP of marketing and we did a cool collaboration together. I guess you never know where a kind gesture and a new connection might lead."

"That's awesome," Rory said. "So how did you go from architecture to marketing?"

"For me, I started to recognize it was the creativity that I really liked. Like I said, ever since I was a kid, I loved to draw.

Designing, creating, making things. I was asking around and someone told me about graphic design, using the computer to design marketing and advertising materials for businesses. I loved the ads in magazines and on TV from my favorite brands. The thought of being able to create those got me really excited. So I did a bunch of research online and ended up taking a graphic design course at the community college where I was taking my other classes. I loved it! That was my first real taste of marketing."

"You ultimately went to work in fashion, right?" Rory asked.

"You've done your homework. Good man! Yep, I ended up finishing my associates degree at the community college in graphic design and went on to NYU. It wasn't totally necessary to go on to a four-year college, but I wanted that experience and knew I could meet a lot of people who could help me in the industry. Ultimately, I had to do an internship to graduate and I got one with a high-end clothing brand. It was crazy. A lot of it was busy work helping them with photoshoots and stuff, but I got to be around all the creative people and see them in action. It confirmed I was going down the right path, that this was what I wanted to be a part of. I got to do a little bit of graphic design for them, touching up images that they put on social media. It was a cool experience."

"It sounds like it," Rory said.

"So that helped me get into the industry. I went to work for someone I met during that internship. Those relationships are invaluable."

"What made you join Elevate?"

"That's an easy one. I saw an opening for the director of marketing position and jumped at it. No pun intended. Haha. The chance to combine my graphic design and marketing skills with my passion for basketball seemed like a dream job. Not to say it's been easy though. It's actually been really hard, but super rewarding."

"I've been hearing that a lot lately," Rory said. "Just because you get into an industry you love doesn't automatically make it easy."

"That's for sure," Damien said. "But it certainly is fun and fulfilling. I wouldn't want to be doing anything else."

"What are some of the coolest things you've been able to do?"

"Well, I've met a lot of high-profile basketball players, including the pro athletes we sponsor. And, because we're at the intersection of fashion and sports, I've met a lot of celebrities at different events. Pretty crazy."

"That would be amazing." Rory was sure Damien could see his jaw drop. *How cool would that be?* His imagination spun out of control. Luckily, he had memorized his questions and kept the interview flowing.

"What other types of jobs are available at a company like Elevate?"

"We have all different kinds of job functions here to make the company run. Much like any company, we have marketing, which I'm the head of. We have finance, human resources, sales, design and manufacturing. It's pretty funny, we have some serious sneaker-heads around here. Even people in the finance department absolutely love shoes and basketball and they've received some cool perks like getting to go to games, industry events and meeting celebrities like me, just from being an employee in the industry."

"That would be amazing!" Rory said. "Damien, what advice would you have for someone like me who wants to get into the basketball industry or even more specifically get a job at a place like Elevate?"

"I want to see that the person is passionate about what we're doing. So I'd want to know that you follow basketball. Basketball players. Teams. Gear. I appreciated that you brought up Jason, one of our athletes. Obviously, you know a little bit about us."

Rory beamed inwardly and did a mental fist pump. *Yes, the homework paid off. Those little connections that mean so much.*

"So showing your passion for the industry in any way you can is important," Damien said. "People want to work with passionate people. Finding ways to stand out is hard, but if you can do something that will impress someone in an interview, that's always good. I once had an interview candidate for a marketing position walk me through their analysis of color theory and trends over the last five years in the shoe industry and where they thought the future was going. They didn't have to prepare that much for an interview, but it certainly made them stand out and I appreciated the effort and the fact that they had an opinion."

Rory scribbled in his notebook.

"I would also tell you to get as much experience as you can," Damien said. "I like to look at a resume and see that they've done things in our field. That could be job shadows, internships or even a summer job in the industry. Show me your hustle. That you want to do what we do. That this is your passion."

"I could talk to you all day," Rory said. "Your passion for what you do is incredible. I can feel it from here. I really appreciate you taking the time today."

"Once you find that passion, it's an unbeatable feeling," Damien said. "People don't believe me, but I can't wait to get to work on Monday morning. That's how much I love this job."

"I sure hope that's me someday soon," Rory said. He swallowed hard and summoned up his courage. "And, Damien, I need to ask. You mentioned job shadows. I'd love to better understand what some of the job functions are on your team. What their day-to-day responsibilities look like and ask them some questions. I certainly don't want to be a bother and could just watch over their shoulder. I guess what I'm saying... is there any chance I could do a job shadow in the Elevate marketing department?"

"I like your style, Rory." Damien said with a hearty laugh. "Going straight in for the ask."

Rory grinned, a little embarrassed.

"Honestly, that's what you gotta do," Damien said. "Let me double check with a few people and maybe we can find a morning that works for everyone. Job shadows don't have to be long. You can learn a lot in a few hours with the team."

"Damien, that would be incredible. Thanks so much."

"It's my pleasure. You should really thank C.J. She put in a good word for you, once again proving the power of networking. And that would be my last bit of advice. You have to reach out to a lot of people, like I did when the people I met on my internship later helped me get into fashion. Those relationships can be key to your own success. It's on you to keep building them."

"I totally get that, Damien. Thank you."

"Right on. I'll check with my team regarding the job shadow and you might end up hearing from one of them to set it up. It was great to meet you over the video chat. Hopefully we can meet in person at the office. Take care, Rory."

"Thanks so much Damien. I really appreciate it. Hope to see you soon."

Rory hung up the video chat and took a deep breath. He'd been nervous for the meeting, but afterward was really thankful he did it. He'd learned some new things and made another contact in the industry. He really hoped he'd hear back from Damien's team. That job shadow would be a great addition to his resume not to mention an awesome learning experience.

seventeen

The Detour is the Path

"Well thanks, Rory, this is a treat," C.J. said.

He'd booked them a table at a Thai place downtown, after pestering that detail out of Reilly

"Well, I have a lot to thank you for," Rory said. "And I thought you might enjoy getting out of the office."

"And one of my favorite restaurants, too. Well done, Rory." She flashed that smile.

"I have so much to tell you," Rory said.

First they ordered, with C.J. asking for five stars of heat on her go-to curry dish.

"First, how's school going?" C.J. asked.

"It's been good, thank you. I made an appointment with my advisor and we talked about what it would take to switch to industrial engineering versus civil engineering. Like you said, it turns out I've taken a lot of the prerequisite classes so the switch isn't too bad. Just to be sure, I did more research on what the day-to-day life of an industrial engineer looks like and how this might translate into the marketing side if I wanted to go that route. I liked what you said about a project manager. Whether in marketing or industrial, it sounds interesting to see a plan through, especially if it has to do with basketball."

"That's great to hear. I'm glad you did the extra research. It's always good to be more informed than less, correct?" C.J. was using her classic, helpful, *You hear me, right?* tone.

"It certainly takes more work, but I understand the benefit." Rory replied.

"So you also had some informational interviews?"

"Yes, I met with Jenny Chen from the Payton University basketball program. She was super nice. I appreciated hearing her story and it sounds like there is someone she wants to introduce me to at a new company that makes smart basketballs. I'm hoping they offer internships. It would be so cool."

"That's great!"

"It's like you've said all along, you have to build these networks of people."

"Exactly. And it sounds like they're paying off." C.J. smiled.

"I sure hope so. Speaking of which, thank you so much for reaching out to Damien. We did an informational video chat and he was really nice. I went out on a limb and even asked him if he'd hook me up with a potential job shadow with his team at Elevate."

"That's great news, Rory. They're doing some cool stuff. I'm sure you'd like that."

"Well, I owe it all to you. If it wasn't for your advice and reaching out then it wouldn't have happened."

"I'm always happy to help, but really it's not me," C.J. said. "Don't discount the fact that *you* put in the work to reach out and meet with these people. *You* made a good impression and *you* asked for the job shadow opportunity. In the end, I can help a little, but it's really up to you."

"I do understand that," Rory said. "It's becoming quite clear that the things I want really are attainable. And that it's on me to put in the hard work and make it happen."

"You're doing all the right things Rory. I'm really glad to see you having such success with it."

Their food arrived and they dug in. Rory was amazed at how C.J. handled the five-star spice level without batting an eye. He had ordered two-star and it still tasted pretty hot to his palate.

"How can you handle that?" Rory said.

"I like my Thai food traditional style," C.J. said. "I spent some time there and learned to appreciate the level of chili they put in. Actually learned to cook my own Thai food."

"Wow, one more thing to admire about you," Rory said. "I'm envious of that traveling, and I'd love to hear more about it."

"Deal," C.J. said. "Remember when I talked about how most people want to find that straight line path ahead in life? Always wanting to be sure to make the right next step. Whether picking your major, finding the right internship or landing the perfect job?"

"Yes, it described me to a T."

"Remember, we also talked about the stress and worry that can come with that?"

Rory nodded. "I sure do."

"It's worth talking about again. You have made some really good decisions that will help you figure out what you want to do. That's important. But I just wanted to remind you that it's okay if you take some detours along the way."

"Detours?"

"Yeah, let me explain. There will be plenty of times on this journey where you have to make some decisions that don't always perfectly align with your long-term vision. Sure, it would be nice to get a paid summer internship in the industry of your choice, and I'm not saying you shouldn't try, but there is a good chance you'll have to take some jobs that just pay the bills because that's what you need. Maybe it's construction or fast food. It's all in how you look at it and can frame it in a future interview."

"What do you mean?" Rory asked.

C.J. stopped to savor another bite of her fiery hot curry.

"When you look at any experience, like a summer job, that might not be aligned with the industry you want to go into, you can still identify the positive qualities you've learned from it. Use construction for example. If you ended up taking a construction job over the summer because it's the best thing you could get, which has nothing to do with basketball, you could still explain that experience in a job interview as something that taught you about the importance of punctuality and hard work. Working at a fast food restaurant is a way of learning the importance of customer service and ensuring customers are happy and satisfied. These are all skills that employers want to know you have and have been cultivated in prior experiences, whether or not they exactly align or not with your industry. Does that make sense?"

"Yes," Rory said. "To quote a wise person I know, No losing, just learning."

She smiled and took another bite.

"Nothing is ever a loss and I shouldn't look at it that way," Rory said. "Every experience has something to learn from and that can be used to my advantage in a future job interview."

"That's exactly right," C.J. said. "Not only is it true, but it's also a healthier way to view this journey and not get stressed out about always choosing the perfect path to the job of your dreams. Like we've talked about, there is no such thing as a perfect path. These kinds of detours can be valuable to who you are becoming."

"That's exactly what I need to hear," Rory said. "It's easy for me to fall into the trap of worrying about always making the right decision to benefit my future."

"And here's where the Thai food comes in," C.J. said. "There is another wonderful kind of detour. It's called travel. You probably know students who backpacked through Europe or went on a mission trip to help people in a foreign country. These experiences can enrich your life and add to your perspective. And yes, they can cost a lot of money, so if you save for a trip, you want to make sure it's worth it to you. And just so I'm clear... I'm not talking about spring break to Florida."

Rory laughed around a mouthful of hot spicy food.

"Employers like to see people who have the courage to go do these things," C.J. said. "People who venture out and explore. Think about sitting in an interview and talking about how navigating through the Andes mountains and meeting the people of Cusco changed how you see yourself and the world. Travel definitely shows you can think bigger and that you'll bring that into your job."

"I haven't done much traveling, but I hope to someday."

"Don't worry, there's plenty of time for that. Yes, it's always enriching to explore another culture. It helps give you empathy and perspective for others."

Rory could sense C.J. getting philosophical again. He waited to let her reflect and finish her food.

"Really, this goes for any experience that shaped you as a human being," she said. "Maybe you volunteered in high school at the local food bank or went to State with the debate team. I'm not saying tell the interviewer every little detail from your life, but if you've had some experiences that have helped you think bigger and changed how you see the world around you and particularly how it pertains to the job, then bring it up in an interview."

Rory finished his own food and put it aside.

"Yum, so good. I can see why you love it," he said. "So why would anyone care about the food bank?"

"Let me explain," C.J. said. "When you think about the job of a hiring manager, you might think that their number-one focus is just to make sure the person they're interviewing can do the work and has the skills and experience required. And if they find the most experienced, most skilled person then they've done their job well. But that's not really the point. Unless the task at hand is done alone in a room with no one else ever around."

Rory laughed.

"Exactly. Not very common. Most jobs require you to interact with other people on the team or at the company. You won't be working alone and the hiring manager wants to be sure you have the right personality and mindset that will fit in and complement the team. So interviews are not only about making sure you explain why you have the right skills to do the job, but also that you have the right attitude and personality. This is why I tell students to be interesting."

"Interesting?"

"Yes, interesting. When you go into a job interview, you want to leave knowing they saw the best parts of you. Not just answer all their specific questions, but share about yourself. Talk about these life experiences that have shaped you. For this very reason, in our job interviews, we ask bigger, broader questions like, *What else are you passionate about?* Or, *What do you like to do for fun?* We want to get to know them as people, not just co-workers."

Rory let it all sink in.

"Okay, I think I get it. Just being able to do the job isn't enough. Letting my personality show is important. Makes sense."

"So let's talk about some of the do's and don'ts of interviewing. Just a few tips to help you when you get the chance. Hopefully you used some of these with Jenny and Damien."

"I'm definitely all ears."

"I know you've probably heard it a thousand times, but first impressions are extremely important. Like it or not, they set the tone for how someone views you. Thankfully, this is something you can control. It starts with your communication when reaching out in the first place. Be kind. Be respectful. Be thoughtful of their time and availability. Before you hit send on an email, reread it three to four times."

"Good, I did that!"

"You've heard me say this before with any communication: spelling errors, like on a resume, can make you look sloppy and unprofessional, like you don't care about the details. You don't want that and you have the chance to correct it. It's usually in our haste, we move too fast and don't take time to proof it. I'm telling you now, look it over multiple times. It can make a huge difference for first impressions."

"I will."

"Once you've made the connection and agreed on a time to meet, be early. Fifteen minutes early is plenty. Likely, that person is busy and will be ready right at the time you scheduled, but being early is a sign of character and respect for that person's time. Of course, the opposite of this is showing up late and that is an absolute sign of disrespect."

Rory cringed inside thinking of the time he was late to see C.J.

"Even if you think you have a good excuse, it just shows you didn't prepare enough to leave early and ensure you make it on time. If you're late to an interview, they might think to themselves, *Will this person be late to work if we hire them? Or late to meetings? Or not get projects done on time?* You don't want anyone having those thoughts about you. So just make sure you get there at least 10 minutes early."

"I can tell these are things that really get under your skin."

"They are! In that effort to be respectful, dressing up is a good idea. Dressing nicer or at least as nice, if they have a more formal office, as the person or people you're meeting with shows respect for them. Yes, this is certainly an older generation thing, but it does show you care about the interview or meeting and I guarantee the person will appreciate it. If you're curious what the dress code is at their office, just call the main telephone number and ask the receptionist. This goes for video interviews as well."

Rory tried to remember what he was wearing when he talked to Damien on the video chat. Thankfully, he remembered it was his favorite blue button-up dress shirt.

"You've heard me say this one before, but it's worth repeating. Always be positive in an interview. Our moms were right: *If you don't have anything nice to say, then don't say anything at all.* Saying negative things about an old boss, or anyone for that matter, just doesn't show well in an interview. Be positive."

Rory thought of a couple of past bosses in particular he didn't like, and made a mental note not to bring them up in interviews.

C.J. wasn't finished. "It's important to be engaging. Too often, I see people interview and only be reactive to the questions. Don't get me wrong, you want to be sure and answer all the questions they have for you, but make it interactive. Ask them questions in return. Do your homework beforehand and research the company. Any new announcements lately? New products or services they launched? Show that you're interested in them and the company. I'm astounded at how many people fail at this. They get to the end of the interview and don't ask any questions. Sounds crazy, but it can really set you apart."

Rory thought about his interview with Damien. He was glad he put those questions together the night before. His research had paid off.

"Also, remember that as much as they're interviewing you, you want to interview them as well," C.J. said. "Make sure you'd be a good fit for the company."

"But what if you just really need the job?"

"Totally understandable, and I've certainly been there early in my career, but if you adopt the practice of being prepared and ask good questions, you will walk out of the interview having put your best foot forward and learned a lot to help you decide if the opportunity is right for you. Some good questions are: What does success look like for this position? How would you describe the culture of the company? What kind of attitudes thrive here? These are general questions that will work for most interviews. They help show you're interested in knowing how to make the most of the opportunity."

Rory definitely took note. He wanted to be sure every interviewer was excited about having him be a part of their team.

The bill arrived at the table, and Rory took it and paid.

"Thank you very much," C.J. said. "It's nice to be treated. Very thoughtful. Now, you might think I'm done, but I've got just a couple more things."

Rory smiled to himself, wondering if it really was only going to be a few more things. He appreciated the fact that C.J. was so passionate about successful interviewing.

"In any job interview, it's natural to want to know about all the benefits the job has to offer. Like how much vacation do you get? Do they offer sick time? Do they contribute to a retirement plan? These are all important things that you'll want to know at some point in order to decide if it's the right job for you. But know that there will always be a chance to learn these things and likely, if they want you to work there, they'll get to those topics at some point. Looking too eager and asking about those in the initial interview can come across like that's all you care about. You don't want them to get the wrong idea. It doesn't always happen that way, but best just to avoid it all together. Don't worry, you'll get the chance to learn those things soon enough. Oh, and lastly, get a good night sleep before your interview. I know, it sounds corny, but you want to be in your best form. You want to be able to show your best self. Believe it or not, I once had a person come interview with me who was hungover."

"Wow!"

"Needless to say, that interview didn't last long. Partly because they needed to run to the restroom halfway through and partly because, well you can figure that one out."

They were both laughing.

"I can't believe someone would show up like that," Rory said.

"It just goes back to how we started this conversation. First impressions matter. As long as you prepare and take it seriously, you'll do just fine."

"I'll take that one to heart," Rory said.

"Well," C.J. said, "I hope you hear back soon from the marketing team at Elevate and also the smart basketball company. I'm sure you can learn a lot from both."

"Thanks C.J. And thanks for all the information today about interviewing. I definitely want to make a good first impression with all my interviews. You never know where they could lead, right? I paid attention to everything you said, and I'll be sure to put it into practice."

"Sounds good, Rory. Looking forward to the updates when I see you next. And hey, thanks for the Thai food. I really enjoyed it."

"My pleasure."

"Oh, by the way, my assistant Reilly was asking me about you the other day." C.J. gave him an extra big smile. "Just thought you'd want to know."

Steps to Take

- Make the most of every job. You're learning valuable skills that can be applied to future jobs.

- Tips when interviewing:
    - First impressions matter
    - Proofread all your communications
    - Be early to the interview
    - Dress up
    - Do your research before on the company and come prepared with questions
    - Be positive (Don't talk negatively about anything)
    - Don't ask about benefits in the first interview
    - Get a good night's sleep the night before (and don't show up hungover!)

/ eighteen /

That Focused Feeling

Rory was early again.

It was a habit that seemed to be increasingly frequent. *I wonder what my old, usually late self would think of me?* He smiled at the thought.

This morning, he'd taken a page straight out of C.J.'s book. He'd risen early, and spent a little time visualizing his new goals and planning his day, then gotten in some pushups and a few stretches. No social media and a quick cold shower.

Now he was a few minutes early for class. It gave him a chance to stand on the steps in front of Ort Hall. He liked the view here. On this crisp, clear day, he could see far down past the Quad and the Virginia Stanton Fountain almost to the end of campus.

He also liked the feeling he had. The physical calm and mental focus. Not in a rush and juggling three things. Clear mind, clear purpose. With this new approach, he was actually finding more to like about his engineering classes. He was also seeing when a fellow classmate was struggling with a concept, and had begun to reach out and lend a hand.

As he stood there, his phone rang. It didn't ring all that often and he didn't recognize the phone number, but he had been waiting for something from the Elevate marketing team.

"Hello."

"Hi, is this Rory Langford?"

"Yes it is."

"Rory, my name is Vanessa Whitaker. I'm the social media manager here at Elevate Footwear. How's it going?"

"Oh hey, it's good. Thanks for calling."

"Of course, do you have a second to chat?"

Rory knew he had to start walking to class soon, but assumed this would only take a moment.

"Yes, absolutely."

"Cool. Well, Damien told me you were interested in learning more about some of our marketing functions here at Elevate. We'd love to have you down to the office for a job shadow with us."

"I would really appreciate that."

"Great. I wanted to reach out and first introduce myself. Damien gave me your email address. I'll shoot you a note and we can find a time that works for both of us. Two to three hours is plenty of time for you to get to see what we do. You can ask as many questions as you want. I hope you don't get bored."

Rory laughed. "I'm sure it will be great. I really appreciate it. Hey, I'm embarrassed to say, but I've already forgotten your name. Can you remind me again?"

"No problem. It's Vanessa. Talk to you soon."

"Thanks again, Vanessa."

And with that call, Rory's day went from great to excellent. Something told him Elevate would be an exciting place to visit. Time to get to class.

That afternoon, as Rory was walking to the study lounge, his phone pinged with the email from Vanessa:

Hi Rory,

Great chatting with you today. How does this Wednesday 9 a.m. to noon or Thursday 2-5 p.m. look to come down for the job shadow?
Please let me know if either of those work. If not, please propose a few times that fit your schedule. I'm sure you're busy with school and we're certainly busy with work, but I know we can find a time to make it happen.

Looking forward to hearing from you,

Vanessa Whitaker
Social Media Manager
Elevate Footwear

Rory felt a tingle of excitement. It was really happening.
Thursday afternoons he didn't have class and 2 p.m. gave him plenty of time to take the bus into the city so he could arrive early. He found a bench, sat down and crafted his reply. He read it multiple times to be sure there were no spelling mistakes or grammatical errors. Like C.J. said, first impressions were everything.
As he continued walking, Rory ran through a mental list of all the new connections he was making. He realized he hadn't heard from Kari Williams, the director of product marketing at DribbleSync. Jenny had said she would make the connection. Maybe he should follow up with Jenny and get her advice on what to do. Maybe she was busy and forgot to send it. Maybe she'd reached out, but Kari was busy. Either way, Rory didn't

want to lose that potential contact. He figured a little investigating and a little nudge was worth it.

He didn't want to pester Jenny, but he remembered what C.J. had said about being kindly persistent and taking responsibility to make things happen. When he got to the study lounge, he found a comfortable, quiet corner and put his full attention into crafting another winning email.

Hello Jenny,

I hope you are doing well. Again, just wanted to say thank you for meeting with me. Also, I wanted to check in regarding the introduction to Kari Williams at DribbleSync. I haven't heard from her, but would still really appreciate the chance to do so.

I hate to bother you about this when you've already been so helpful. And I'd be happy to contact her myself if you want to send me her information and that works better for you. Please let me know what you think the best direction is to take.

Thanks again for everything. Hope you have an excellent season.

Go Wildcats,

Rory
rory.langford@payton.edu
555-555-4971

He cracked open an engineering textbook and began to study. Next time he checked his phone, he was surprised to find that Jenny had already replied.

Hi Rory,

Great to hear from you. I've been well, thanks for asking.

I did chat with Kari a little while back about connecting with you, but I know she is a very busy woman. It probably wouldn't hurt to send her an email introducing yourself as the person I mentioned. Sometimes we all get busy and things can fall off our to-do list. It happens. I don't think she would mind hearing from you at all.

Her email is kari.williams@dribblesync.com. This is probably the best way to reach her.

Let me know if there is anything else I can help you with.

Best of luck!!

Jenny

Wow! For the second time today, Rory felt a rush of excitement through his body. It was that feeling he remembered from game day, as the team went through their warm up drills and the gym began to fill with fans. His mom watching. Except in this game day replay, he found Emma's face replaced with Reilly's.

Time to write another email. These were becoming easier the more of them he wrote. And this time, Rory felt he had two big advantages: Kari's direct email, and the fact that Jenny had already introduced him.

He took the time and crafted his email, making sure to mention Jenny. He also was a bit more specific about what he wanted to discuss with Kari. Not only did he want to talk about jobs in basketball, but he was also curious to know if DribbleSync offered internships. After reading it multiple times and checking his grammar and spelling, he sent it off.

Then he took a break and looked up Reilly on social media. He couldn't find her anywhere.

nineteen

Jumping Higher

Thursday couldn't come soon enough. Rory woke up with a feeling of eager anticipation. Today he would head to Elevate headquarters to meet with the social media team.

He took the bus into the city and headed to the east end of town. The building looked more like an old rundown warehouse than the office setting he was expecting. When he opened the door he was surprised to see the inside had been completely renovated. The flooring looked like an old basketball gym, lines and all. The office was open and natural light poured in from the skylights on the roof.

Rory saw a reception desk and some seats that looked like old wood bleacher seats in a gym. Past that was a glass-walled conference room where seven or eight people were meeting.

Rory checked his phone. *Ten minutes early. Perfect.*

No one was sitting at the reception desk so he sat down on one of the bleachers. There was basketball memorabilia on the walls, including photos of some of the biggest names in the game. There were also lots of shoes on display. Even though Elevate was a relatively new brand, Rory had seen their lines over the last few years.

He got up and walked closer. Next to each shoe was a date and some details. It looked like the date each shoe had been released and its technological advancements. Some listed the pro player who wore them.

Rory checked his phone again. He looked back at the reception desk; still nobody. He was worried that Vanessa would think he was late. He thought about emailing her. As he looked closer, he saw a sign that said *Check In*. He walked over and saw what looked to be a digital tablet on the counter. *Please search for who you're here to see and we'll reach out and let them know you're in the lobby.*

It finally dawned on Rory that no one was coming out. No problem. He typed in Vanessa's name and found her in the directory. He clicked the *I'm Here* button. A screen appeared saying, *Thank you, we've let them know.* Rory sat back down and waited.

Not two minutes later, a short, lively woman in her mid-twenties came out to the lobby. She had sandy blonde hair with bright red streaks in it.

"Hey, what's up? You must be Rory!" she said. "I'm Vanessa. Nice to meet you."

"Hi Vanessa," Rory said. "It's a pleasure to meet you too. Thanks so much for having me down to the office."

"You bet. We've got a fun little afternoon planned. But first, let me give you the grand tour and introduce you to some of the others on the team."

"That would be great."

"All right," she said. "Follow me." She waved in the direction past the glass conference room and started down the hall.

It was a bit like C.J.'s office. Music was playing throughout and you could feel the energy. Some people were at their desks working. Others were in common areas talking to each other.

"First things first, here's the kitchen." She pointed to the right. Against the wall were two fridges, a counter and a sink with an island in front of it. "Of course, all the juice, pop and sparkling water you could ever want. You thirsty?"

"I'm okay, thanks."

"Chips, energy bars, apple? Lemonheads candy? We're going to be busy this afternoon." She had a bit of a *Don't-say-I-didn't-warn-you* tone.

"Ha! I think I'm good, but thank you."

"Okay, here we go. Over in that corner is the finance team. Just next to them is our human resources department. And back in that corner is the product development group. That's where the real magic happens."

Rory noticed that area looked more private and closed off.

"Hey Vanessa, why is that part of the office not as open as the rest?"

"Oh, we're pretty secretive about product innovation and the newest lines coming out at Elevate. They keep it buttoned up. You actually have to have special access to get through that frosted glass door right there. Top-secret clearance. Retinal scan. Pentagon-type stuff."

She sounded serious and Rory didn't know what to think. She saw his face and laughed.

"I'm just kidding," she said. "Well sort of. Innovation *is* a really big deal around here so they keep it pretty locked down. I've only been back there twice."

Wow. Now that would be cool.

"Those doors lead to our other building. We're lucky enough to have our own workout room, locker rooms and a gym. We'll be going there later. Right now let's head upstairs so you can meet the rest of the team."

They climbed the stairs to the second floor. Vanessa gestured with two hands, as if she was guiding an airplane along a tarmac.

"Over there is our sponsorship team and the sales team and down that way are the executive offices. Our CEO is in that office at the end."

The interior design was sleek and modern, with more glass walls and clean lines. Rory liked that style.

"And over here is the marketing team. I think you know this guy."

As they arrived, she pointed to a desk in the front. And there was Damien, looking as sharp as ever.

"Hey Rory, great to see you in person. You're a little taller than in your video chats."

They laughed.

"Cool place." Rory said.

"Yeah, we like it. I'm glad Vanessa could give you the grand tour. Did she force the Lemonheads on you?"

"Uh yeah...I mean…"

"Just kidding. She loves Lemonheads."

"Hey, they're good!" Vanessa said. "Anyway… over here is Misha, she's an art director on our team. She's primarily our lead designer for all marketing efforts, but she's an awesome Swiss Army knife who does it all. She takes most of our photos for social, designs all posts and even writes copy if we need it. We'd be lost without her."

"Awe, thanks Vanessa. Nice to meet you, Rory," Misha said.

"And rounding out our small, but mighty team over here is Octavio. He's our social media specialist. He helps me with strategy, posts and placements and anything else to keep things rolling. He's awesome."

"That's kind Vanessa, thanks," Octavio said. "Great to meet you Rory. I hope we can impart a little wisdom on you today."

"Honestly, I'm just happy to be here. You're all living the dream as far as I can tell. Working for a cool company in a cool industry. It's exactly where I want to go."

"It's not *all* fireworks and lollipops everyday," Damien said.

The team all looked at him.

"You know what I mean. I'm just saying there is a lot of hard work in what we do. Even when you find something you really love, you have to remember there will be good days and bad days. You don't want to set yourself up thinking you're going to love every single minute of it. But I do appreciate your enthusiasm, Rory. Sometimes I need a reminder that we do work in an awesome industry with some really great people."

"Well, that got deep fast," Misha said.

Damien laughed. "All right, back to it. I know you guys have work to do this afternoon."

Vanessa motioned to the team for all of them to go sit down on the couches in the corner of the room.

"Let's share our plan with Rory for what we're doing this afternoon," she said.

Vanessa, Misha, Octavio and Rory all walked over and sat down. Vanessa started the conversation.

"So one of the things we're always doing on the social media team is creating content for our different channels," she said. "It's important we're always showcasing our products. We thought it'd be fun to go take some photos of a couple pairs of our newest shoes. We were thinking of some shots in our own gym, but also getting out into the city and finding some cool places. You down Rory?"

"Yeah, absolutely."

"Would you be cool being the model?" Vanessa asked.

"Wait, what?" The team all paused and were staring at him.

"Don't worry, all the shots will be from the knee down."

They all laughed as Rory's visible apprehension instantly melted away and a smile came back to his face.

"What size shoe do you wear?" Vanessa asked.

"Eleven and a half."

"Alright. Octavio, can you grab those for us?"

"No problem."

"Great, Misha will get the photo gear and we'll head out."

For the next three hours, Rory got to see the Elevate social media team in action. They took lots of different photos in different locations, including an outdoor court, indoor court and just hanging out in the park. Misha and Vanessa had a vision for what they wanted to get based on a plan that Octavio had put together. It was really great to work together with this team. His favorite part was when he got to jump as high as he could for a shot of the shoes in action. Everyone egged him on to jump higher. That was a rush. He felt like an important part of the project, working with others to achieve a goal, and he loved it. Almost better than game day. And those shoes felt amazing on his feet.

In between shoots, Rory peppered each of the team members with questions about their job, background and education. And he made sure to ask for their best piece of advice.

Vanessa said, "Sample different jobs. That could be job shadows, internships/apprenticeships or real jobs themselves. It's hard to know exactly what you're going to like. In time, you'll have more experiences to draw from and be able to hone in on the job that gives you the most fulfillment."

Misha told him, "Really work your network. I really wanted to be in fashion. I asked everyone I knew if they had any connections to the fashion industry. It sounds random, but it was a friend of my aunt's who was working at Elevate in the accounting department. I reached out to her and she introduced me to Damien. You have to be proactive if it's what you want."

Octavio said, "It's okay to take an entry-level job or maybe not the exact job you were hoping for in an effort to get in and make connections. Once you get in, work hard and prove yourself to be valuable to the company, and they'll likely recognize it. I started in the Elevate warehouse two years ago. I worked really hard. I was always on time, I gave 110 percent and that allowed me to look for other jobs within the company and get a great recommendation from my supervisor to go into this role."

The afternoon went by way too fast, and they were back at the office.

"Hey, where's Damien? I'd love to thank him in person."

Vanessa pointed to the top secret room.

"Well, thank you Vanessa, Misha and Octavio," he said. "I had a blast."

"And you were really good to work with," Misha said. "We love your enthusiasm and you can jump pretty high too."

Rory felt a warm glow.

"Now those shoes…" Octavio said.

"Yeah, right, almost forgot," Rory said. He bent down to take them off.

"Wear them," Octavio said. "You're now our newest brand ambassador."

No way.

"I absolutely cannot thank you all enough," Rory said. "I don't want to leave."

As he left, Rory stepped along quite smartly on his new shoes. He hummed a tune to himself and felt his heart might burst with happiness. That was an incredible feeling. He was already composing thank-you notes to each of the Elevate team members in his head.

What would he do the rest of the day? Xavier had invited him to someone's house to watch a big game. Sometimes in the past Rory had needed that crowd around him to feel good. Or if he wasn't in the mood, he would have retreated to his own space, to slump somewhere with his phone and watch other people's lives scroll by with the brush of his thumb on his sports, social and entertainment feeds.

Not today.

He knew a place in town where kids played pickup ball. He headed that direction instead.

Let's see what these new shoes can do.

/ twenty /

Sweet Rewards

It's amazing what some fresh air, sunshine and physical activity will do. And having a purpose in your step. And wearing new shoes.

Rory slept like a rock that night. He didn't look at his phone before bed, a first. He didn't even hear Xavier come in late.

When he woke, stretched and planned his day, it felt like the beginning of a new life.

If you could put this feeling in a jar, everyone would want some.

When he finally did check his phone, there were three very good things waiting, his sweet reward for all the work and discipline.

The first was a text from an unknown number. It said, *Check out the new campaign on Insta. Cheers, Octavio.*

He looked up the Elevate Instagram account, and his heart leaped. There were his new shoes, jumping so high in the air you couldn't see the ground. The sun came through the shot and it looked amazing, like a major ad campaign. *Those were his feet! That was his jump!* He wished the world could see. He wished Reilly could see. While Xavier snored away in his bunk, Rory screenshotted the picture and texted it to his mom.

The second very good thing was a voicemail.

"Rory, this is Reilly. Really good to hear from you. I'm just catching up and got your message. Yes, you are confirmed with C.J. and we'll see you soon. I hope you have a great day."

Her voice sounded so good that Rory listened to her voicemail three times.

How much better could the day get?

Well, the trifecta was an email from Kari at DribbleSync. She apologized for the delay in connecting and was open for an informational interview over the phone. Rory would have preferred to have it in person, but he also knew he should take whatever he could get. He responded and set up a time for the call.

In his new spirit of being early and overprepared, he went to work right then and there. He Googled DribbleSync and read up on all their products including the latest release, a product called the DS4. He checked out and followed all their social media feeds. As he read, he found himself really impressed with the product. He liked how the company presented itself. This looked like the kind of company he wanted to work for.

He prepared a list of questions for Kari, mostly about her own education and work journey. He also added a couple questions about DribbleSync's future plans. To be extra sure he didn't forget to ask about summer internships, he highlighted his last question with a green highlighter. He rehearsed his questions a few times.

When the time came, he was ready. He put in his ear buds and dialed the number.

"Thanks for calling DribbleSync, this is Alex. How may I help you?"

"This is Rory Langford, and I have a call scheduled with Kari Williams."

"Just a moment please… Okay, here you go."

"Thanks."

"Hello, this is Kari Williams."

"Hi Kari, this is Rory Langford. It's nice to meet you by phone. I hope now is still a good time for this informational interview?"

"Absolutely, Rory. Thanks for calling." Kari had a calming, inviting voice.

"I just want you to know I really appreciate you taking time out of your day to talk with me." Rory said.

"Well, Jenny at Payton is a good friend and customer, so if she says nice things about you then I'm in."

Rory laughed.

"Sorry it had to be over the phone," Kari said. "This is a really busy season for us and I wasn't sure if I could make time to meet in person."

"Not a problem at all. Again, I'm just grateful for your time. Should we dive in?"

"Sounds good."

Rory looked at the questions he'd prepared. "I was hoping you could tell me a little about your own path. What did you do for school? What were some of the other jobs you had before coming to work at DribbleSync?"

"Sure," Kari said. "I had no clue what I wanted to do when I graduated high school, but I figured some sort of degree after high school would be beneficial. I didn't have the money to attend a four-year university. The local community college was a good option to get some core prerequisites done and test out a few classes in what I thought I might like. One of the English credit options was a technical writing class."

"What exactly is technical writing?"

"It's the instructional content you'd find in a manual explaining how to use a product. Or the product details on a website explaining how the product or service works. I liked it, because it was just the facts, plain and simple. Like two plus two equals four. That's kind of how my brain works. I took a few personality tests in high school and it was important to me to find something professionally that aligned with my skills and personality traits. I think job satisfaction comes when you're doing work that is right for who you are. Understanding yourself better can help with that."

"I'm working on that myself," Rory said. "I've taken a couple of personality tests, but this is a good reminder to do more."

"You'll be glad you did," Kari said. "To continue answering your question, I finished community college and started looking for work. To this day I still regret not seeking out internship opportunities while I was still in school. It's such a good way to meet people in the industry and grow your network."

Rory smiled. He was definitely seeing a pattern in hearing the same advice over and over.

"I ended up getting a job for a really big software company writing their instructional content on how to best use their product," Kari said. "I learned a lot, but I found that I didn't love working for a large corporation. After about four years, I decided I was ready for something else. I wanted to challenge myself a bit more too. When I stopped and asked myself what I really wanted to do, I realized that I wanted to help people be active. I loved paddleboarding and hiking and I thought it would be more fulfilling to work for a company that promoted that kind of lifestyle."

"That's cool that you stopped to recognize it," Rory said.

"I appreciate you saying that," Kari said. "I think it's important to be reflective along your journey to ensure you're aligned with your true self."

Rory wondered if Kari had received advice from C.J.

"Up to that point, most of the work I'd been doing was technical writing, but every once in a while, the marketing department needed me to do some copywriting. It was fun to challenge myself and use my writing to help sell the product and not just explain how to use it after they'd bought it. So I combined my interest in getting people more active with the challenge of marketing and I started looking at product marketing jobs. I ended up finding an interesting opportunity in product marketing with an electric bicycle manufacturer called BlueLine."

"Aren't they based in Seattle?"

"They are. I ended up moving there for the job. Even though I'm from here, it was a really fun adventure to try a new city, meet new people and spread my wings a bit."

"That takes a lot of guts," Rory said. "I admire that."

"I was only twenty-five at the time. It was a really great learning experience for me. I'd recommend it to anyone."

"How long did you live there?"

"I was in Seattle for five years, and I worked at BlueLine the whole time. It was great. Not only did I learn a lot about product marketing, I was also able to get out and explore. I went hiking and camping and paddleboarding in the Puget Sound. Unfortunately, they ran out of money and the company had to close. Things don't always turn out the way you'd hoped, right?"

"Oh wow. That must have been hard. You'd moved all the way out there for the job."

"I don't regret a thing." Kari said. She sounded like she had a confident, optimistic disposition. That growth mindset. "I'd met some really great people in Seattle, so I reached out to all my contacts. Someone introduced me to a large engineering design software company in the area. Even though I had some trepidation about going back to work for a large company, I did it anyway. Honestly, after BlueLine failed, I just needed a job to pay the bills. It was a good company with nice people, but I still wanted that smaller company culture. I stayed for a year, then decided I wanted something else."

"So what did you do?"

"Well, I got self-reflective again. I realized I had gotten away from the things I'd really wanted. I needed to get aligned."

Rory laughed again under his breath. More advice he kept hearing over and over.

"I decided I wanted to move back to this area," Kari said. "I wanted to get back to a smaller company that was helping people be active. I tried using LinkedIn and working my network, but nobody was really connected to anything that interested me. So, believe it or not, I started doing exactly what you're doing. I started reaching out and asking for informational interviews at companies I might want to work for."

"Nice!"

"It was a little bit like starting from scratch, but it helped me build relationships and have them get to know me. They could put a name to a face and a personality and it got me further along than the others. I ended up interviewing with three different companies and getting this opportunity at DribbleSync. I found I was excited about their product, I really enjoyed the people I'd met and the company's values aligned with mine."

"It's good to hear these tactics are not just something that works during college." Rory said.

"I think all three of those companies appreciated how proactive I was about learning about them. That I was taking the time to make sure it was a good fit for me, too. So many people just send in resumes or apply on a jobsite and hope that is enough to get an interview. Sometimes it is, but it helps to show that extra effort. And now I've been here for four years."

"So what do you love about working at DribbleSync?"

"I definitely like working for an innovative technology company. We're always trying to bring the very best experience to our customers. It's great working for a company so committed to that."

"What don't you like about it?"

"Always a good question," Kari said. "And I think this is true with any company, but sometimes people can be very strong in their opinions and what they want. That can be challenging. I've learned over the years that you need to have healthy confrontation with people to get to a better outcome."

"What do you mean, healthy confrontation?"

"Oftentimes, when people have issues with each other, they don't say anything. They just stew on it and quietly get more angry. This doesn't help anyone. At BlueLine, I had a boss who called it healthy confrontation. It just meant recognizing when there was an issue between us and that we need to respectfully approach one another and discuss the issue. Quite often we could get a better understanding of where the other was coming from and collectively resolve the issue. It was all about not being mean, not being petty, but being committed to working well together. I've always appreciated that approach and now I use it with my team at DribbleSync."

"That makes total sense," Rory said. "It seems like a better way of dealing with things."

"We certainly think so. It makes for a better team culture and that's really important to the success of any company."

"So as the director of product marketing, what do you do?"

"Our department works on all the product details. My team ensures that consumers understand the benefits of our products. So we create marketing content for product packaging, the website, our companion app, social media and video projects. Our team has writers, analysts and project managers. They're all passionate about health, fitness and particularly basketball. A few of us even got to go to the NBA All-Star game last year. It was fantastic."

"That would be a dream come true for me."

"There are a lot of fun perks that come with this job, that's for sure."

"I'm getting an industrial engineering degree, but ultimately, I think I want to get into some sort of product marketing role," Rory said. "Do you think my degree will help?"

"Actually, yes. Understanding how things work is a great background for explaining it to others. And industrial engineering is challenging, so it shows you're up for doing tough things. I think that could be really good for you."

"That's excellent to hear. I really appreciate you taking this time with me, Kari, and I only have a couple more questions, out of respect for your time. What advice would you give someone like me who is interested in getting into this industry?"

"Well Rory, it's a pleasure to talk to you. You're making connections already and that's probably one of the most important things. I would also say, be flexible. I've had some interesting jobs along the way and learned from each one. Not every opportunity is going to be your dream job in your dream industry. And that's okay. Like I said earlier, be reflective and ask yourself what you're liking and what you're not. Are you growing, learning and expanding your responsibilities? Is the work fulfilling? Why or why not? For most of us, it takes a lot of experiences to narrow it down. That's fine. As humans, we change as we grow. What you once really liked might not be what you like today. And that's okay too. Be open to change."

"Wow, thanks Kari. I like how you put that. Great advice." Rory scribbled in his notebook.

"It did sound good, didn't it? I should have written that down," Kari said.

"I actually did. I'll be sure to send you the highlights."

They laughed.

"Hey, before I forget, I wanted to ask you one other thing. Is DribbleSync doing any internships this summer? I would really love to work in a department like yours for a company like that."

"That's nice to hear you say, Rory. Yes, we actually do have a couple spots for a product marketing internship this summer. I can't promise anything and you'll have to apply like everyone else, but I really hope you do."

On his end of the call, Rory stood up and did a few silent fist pumps into the air.

"I most definitely will," he said.

"It would be fun to talk to you more about it. We will be posting information about it on our website very soon, so keep an eye out."

"Absolutely. And thanks again for taking the time to chat with me. It means a lot. I hope we get the chance to talk more. Watch for my internship application."

"I certainly will, Rory. Thanks for reaching out, and best of luck to you."

After making sure he'd ended the call, Rory leaped to his feet.

"YeahOOOO!"

It was loud enough they could probably hear him across campus.

Then he jumped as high as he could into the air, just to test out his brand new shoes.

/ twenty-one /

The Strangest Encounter

Rory was thrilled about the prospects for an internship with DribbleSync. But he knew he couldn't only count on that. Like Kari said, he'd have to apply like everyone else, and he could only assume that other people with strong educational backgrounds and experiences would apply as well. He wondered how many of them had talked to Kari or someone else at the company. Even though right now this was his first choice, he decided to look for other internships to improve his chances.

He'd seen an ad in the university newspaper for a new startup looking for interns, a company called ShareDrive. They had created an app that allowed users to rent out their cars to others when they weren't using it as a way to make a little extra money. It wasn't exactly in his preferred industry, but he was willing to do it for free in an effort to gain experience and grow his network. If it worked with his schedule, he was hoping he could fit it in during spring semester every Tuesday and Thursday afternoon for a few hours.

Rory emailed ShareDrive and they got back to him pretty quickly and said they'd love to talk. Rory had worked on his resume and made sure he brought three copies. He'd already emailed it to them, but he wanted to be prepared if anyone he met with hadn't seen it yet.

When he arrived, ShareDrive's office looked small and a little dated, but Rory expected that for a young company. There were no chairs and no receptionist. Someone walked past.

"Hi, I'm here for a 2 p.m. internship interview," Rory said.

"Ah, okay, I'll tell Sean. Sorry there's no place to sit. We don't have chairs yet in the lobby."

Rory didn't mind standing. He was early and figured he'd have to wait a little bit. To his surprise, that ended up being more than 45 minutes. At 2:40 p.m., someone finally came into the lobby.

"Hey, remind me of your name again."

"Oh sure, I'm Rory Langford."

"Ah, okay. I'm Sean Mason, the CEO of ShareDrive." Sean didn't look much older than 25. His clothes were wrinkled as if he'd been wearing them for a few days now. His tired eyes told the same story.

"Nice meeting you, Mr. Mason. Thanks for taking the time to catch up with me."

"Well, if you can help us grow this thing fast and we don't have to pay you, then no need to thank me."

Rory was surprised and didn't know what to say. He just smiled and nodded.

"Let's go to the conference room over here," Sean gestured to the door on the opposite side of the lobby. This room was shabby too. When they sat down, Rory's chair was wobbly. Sean looked at Rory through those tired eyes and asked in a sort of monotone, "So why are you here?"

"Oh, well, I saw your ad looking for interns. I'd love to help and I emailed my resume. Did you happen to see it?"

"Dude, I work 80 hours a week trying to get this app off the ground," Sean said. "I haven't had time to look at any intern resumes."

Again, Rory didn't know what to say. He remembered he'd brought a few copies.

"No problem," he said. "I have one here for you."

Sean took the resume from Rory and stared at it for an uncomfortable amount of time.

"Am I missing something?" he said in that flat tone of voice. "Looks like you're getting an industrial engineering degree. Is that right?"

His skeptical tone put Rory back on his heels.

"Yes, that's right. I was hoping I could help out with your company's marketing efforts. Although I'm getting an engineering degree, I hope to minor in marketing and get into the product marketing field."

"But you have zero marketing experience? What did you think you could even do for us?"

This interview was stranger than all the rest. Rory tried to think quickly. He kept his voice tempered despite his mounting frustration.

"Well, several things," he said. "I think I could help you with any sort of research you might need on better understanding your customers. I could also help with writing social media posts or any sort of product information for the app or your website. I'm willing to jump in wherever you need some extra help. I know I don't have a lot of experience, but I do think I could add value. If you have concerns, you or someone else could always review my work before anything goes live."

Sean's face showed impatience.

"Honestly, I don't have time for that, Cory," he said, getting his name wrong. "We need people that can jump in and do the work themselves. I can't babysit anyone."

Rory sat stunned. He tried to hide his confusion. *Wasn't this an internship? An opportunity for students to learn from the company and its employees?* He figured they knew he wouldn't have all the answers and they would be willing to help him along the way.

"Have you had interns here before at ShareDrive?" he asked.

"Nope, never," Sean said. "But since we can't afford any employees, we're hoping some unpaid marketing interns could do the work."

"I see.'

"At least some interns with more experience," Sean said in a condescending tone.

As Sean stared at him and tapped impatiently on the table, Rory took stock of his situation. It was clear this wasn't a good fit. He wasn't what Sean was looking for, but more importantly, he did not want to volunteer his time for a guy like that. It was time to go.

"Sean, I'm sorry I wasn't exactly what you were looking for," Rory said in a kind, calm voice. "And I wish you and ShareDrive the best of luck." He stood up.

"Yeah, uh, thanks man." Sean was already looking down at his phone as Rory walked out.

Well that was strange and uncomfortable, Rory thought on his way back to campus. *What went wrong? Was it me?*

He got a hunger pang and realized he'd been too excited to eat. Now he felt hollow, somehow embarrassed and low on confidence. It was the opposite of the elation he'd had when he got off the phone with Kari at DribbleSync.

Luckily, his next appointment with C.J. was tomorrow. He needed his mentor's take on this strange turn in his quest for purpose.

/ twenty-two /

You Can't Win 'Em All

All morning Rory had wondered if he would see Reilly this time. And here she was right in front of him. And once again, he didn't have anything clever to say.

"Hello, Rory. I see you're early as usual." Her voice was like honey and her eyes sparkled.

He wanted to tell her all the things that were working so well in his life right now, but instead something else came out of his mouth.

"Do you wanna see my shoes?"

He was embarrassed for himself as soon as he said it.

"Sure, Rory, let's see your shoes." She said it in such a nice way, like they were in on the same joke.

He stepped around to the side of her desk and she let out a whistle, another admirable trait.

"Fancy!"

"I was a shoe model with Elevate one day, and they even put some of the pictures on Instagram."

"Shoe model, huh?" Reilly raised one eyebrow.

"It was… it was great." Rory said. All his words seemed to have mysteriously vanished. "Um, is C.J. in?"

"You have an appointment, don't you?" she teased. "I'll walk you back."

It was a walk he wished could have lasted forever, but was over in a flash.

"Have a good chat, Rory," Reilly said. "I hear you're killing it." She walked away. His heart leaped.

"Rory!" C.J. said. She glanced significantly in the direction of the departing Reilly.

"Come in and give me your update," C.J. said. "It's been too long."

"Yes, you were traveling," Rory said, still thinking about Reilly. "How was the trip?"

"East Coast," C.J. said. "Very good trip. Some business, some sightseeing. Thanks for asking. Now I'm excited to hear about all your recent developments."

"I'm so glad you asked," Rory said. "I've got a strange one for you. I need your help understanding it."

"Yes?"

Rory explained his experience with Sean and ShareDrive.

"I thought I'd done everything right," he said. "But I walked out of there pretty confused with how it all went down."

"Aw, Rory. I'm really sorry you had to experience that. I hate to say it, but that's just part of the journey. Sooner or later you're going to come across those types of people in interviews, as team members or even as a manager. I've heard some pretty weird things in interviews myself. I once had someone tell me I wasn't humble enough to get the job."

"You? Not humble enough?"

"Right? Sometimes people misperceive us, prejudge us, or in your case, are even a bit rude. It happens. Try not to let it get you down. Keep that growth mindset and move on."

"I appreciate that perspective, C.J. Will do."

"So tell me. How's the rest of it been going?"

"Just like you told me, I've been doing the Design and Exploration parts of the IDEAS Framework in tandem. It's really exciting. I've been finding companies, reaching out and setting up initial conversations, *and* going out and seeing them. I can't believe I'm actually doing it."

This seemed to please C.J. immensely. "I knew you had it in you," she said with a smile.

"The job shadow at Elevate was really cool. I got to see a day in the life and met some really amazing people. They actually pulled me in on a photo shoot and I got to wear their newest pair. Check them out! The marketing side can be really fun."

"Nice shoes! And I love that you got that experience. Isn't it amazing working with a good team of creative people?"

"I loved it," Rory said.

"And what about your connection to the smart basketball company?"

"DribbleSync? That went well. I think product marketing could really fit me. I can blend my love of how things work with the fun of marketing. And Kari had some really good insights. They do have internship opportunities this summer that I'm going to apply for."

"Very good. I've got a little tip for you that might increase your chances of standing out."

"I'm all ears."

"Well, considering that many people just do the bare minimum when applying for a job or internship, it doesn't take much to stand out. So get creative."

"What do you mean?"

"Well, it's just an idea, but what if you made a video? You could film yourself doing a review of one of DribbleSync's products. Or create two or three short videos that could be used on social media. Almost like the photo shoot you did with the Elevate team. Using your own phone would be fine. It's not to say they'll actually use it, but again, it shows extra effort. It demonstrates that you're not just going to do the minimum."

"For sure. I could do that." Rory already had some ideas.

"Or it could also be as simple as a video of you talking about your background and why you want the summer internship. Sending in a video or two is unique and different and I'm sure will be appreciated by those choosing the summer interns. It also gives you a chance to showcase your personality. It's great that you chatted with Kari, but there are probably others involved with the selection process."

"Those are great. Yes, I want to stand out. I really want that internship."

"Take some time to think about it. Be creative. Probably not a bad idea to bounce it off a few people and see what they think. You don't want to come off cheesy, right?" They both laughed.

"No I don't." Rory said. "I'll keep it professional, like something I'd create if I was working for them."

"That's a good lens to be looking through. And you should definitely be seeking out some other summer internship opportunities, too. Never put all your eggs in one basket, right?"

"I totally agree. I'm researching others."

"That's good. Now I want to share with you the second-to-last phase in the IDEAS Framework: Adaptability. This phase is all about reflecting on your time in the Design and Exploration phases. What did you like? What did you not like? What did you think of the working environments? What did you think of the management style of the people you shadowed and interned with? What part of the work did you find most interesting? What surprised you? Is this still an industry you're interested in? If so, is there value in researching other job types in this industry? If not, is it time to bring up your notes from the

Introspection phase and see what other industries might be worth learning more about?"

Rory nodded in agreement. He was taking notes.

"It's pretty typical of most of us to have preconceived notions of what we think things are going to be like or what we think will be most aligned with us. But it's important to be reflective to see if we were right or if we learned something new along the way. This is where that growth mindset comes back into play. Do you truly believe that you can learn from your experiences and have the humility to let them shape you? Truth is, you might be wrong in your initial decisions. You might not like a certain major you were considering or job type that you were originally researching or *even* the industry that you thought you were most passionate about. That's all okay. The key is recognizing it and being able to adapt to something new. Again, it's accepting the winding path, right?"

"That seems scary. I hate being wrong," Rory said.

"Yes, but being wrong is so valuable and constructive on your way to truly being more like you."

"I get it."

"It's important in this phase to journal your findings. This can be written down in your notebook or on your phone, but somewhere you can look back and reflect on your thoughts. If you're really being diligent, you'd make time after every informational interview, job shadow or internship to write down the pros and cons of each experience. That way it's fresh in your mind and will be the truest reflection of your feelings."

"Oh, I've got some work to do then." Rory said.

C.J. laughed. "It's not just the act of doing it, but a mindset. Be okay with learning, adapting and pivoting when necessary. Letting that reflection shape your future decisions and actions will be incredibly useful to you finding purpose, fulfillment and happiness along your professional journey."

"I'm committed to doing that. And C.J., I can never thank you enough."

"Rory, my time is my gift to you. I am very impressed at how you've taken the IDEAS Framework and run with it. You are fast becoming my star pupil. You are on your way to great things and making your mother very proud."

She has such a good, honest way of building me up, Rory thought. *That in itself is an art I am going to master.*

"Speaking of the path, we're getting closer to the end of our sessions together, you know."

"I know and I'm not happy about it," Rory mock-pouted.

"Ha! Time to turn you loose to go and do some good of your own," C.J. said. "But right now, there are three important personal practices that I wanted to be sure I shared with you. They have all been foundational to my own health and happiness and I want you to consider them for yourself."

Again, as he so often did with C.J., Rory found himself leaning in and listening a bit more intently.

"The first is regular exercise," C.J. said.

"Yes, I still remember the core workout from hell," Rory said.

"Right! You're welcome back for round two at my gym anytime," she said with a wink. "We've all heard about the importance of getting exercise, but too often the busyness of life gets in the way, especially when you join the working world, and you just don't make it a priority anymore. Aside from just being in better physical shape and having more energy to do things, it's also a really great stress reliever. And honestly, I don't care how much you love your job, it still can get stressful."

"What about playing basketball?"

"Absolutely. Walking, running, yoga, spin, bootcamp or whatever. Make it fun. Do it with other people. Just as long as you're regularly doing it to get the benefits."

"I agree with that. I just have to remember to do it," Rory said "Life gets busy and I tend to forget."

"That's typical for most of us. You just have to make it a priority and a habit. But do it. It's so good for you in so many ways. The next thing I wanted to share with you is the benefits of meditation."

"Meditation?"

"I know it sounds goofy, but I started meditating after I heard it was a regular practice for many high-achieving people. It's a game changer. I've really enjoyed the benefits."

"What kind of benefits?"

"Much like exercise, it can be a really amazing stress reliever. When I find myself feeling stressed, which for me is often felt in my shoulders, I find time to close my office door or find a quiet room and I use a meditation app on my phone. Relaxing and focusing on my breathing can really help reduce the tension. More and more studies are finding how dangerous stress can be on the human body. Obviously, reducing it can help tremendously."

"I don't know. I think I'd rather just sit and watch SportsCenter."

"I understand your hesitancy. A lot of people feel that way before they try it. But once you do, you will see the benefits. It takes some getting used to and they don't have to be long sessions to reap the rewards. Sitting quiet for even 10 minutes at a time can feel weird. You have to practice. One of the biggest benefits for me is the increased focus. With a million different things trying to get our attention at any given moment, like our phones, email, co-workers and family, it's nice to be able to train your brain to focus on one thing. I use it a lot at night if I wake up with a lot of things on my mind. It allows me to calm my thoughts and fall back asleep."

"I always have a hard time falling back asleep at night because I'm thinking of all the things I have to do the next day," Rory said. "I hate that."

"Exactly. Well, then you'll love this practice," C.J. said. "You'll learn to relax and focus your thoughts on a single thing. I've really found it helpful and I think you should at least give it a try."

"If you say so." Rory said with a half smile.

She laughed. "Ok, the last one might be the most important. It's about embracing gratitude."

Rory felt himself rolling his eyes. "What are you trying to do, turn me into a monk?"

"No monk, just a better human. This is about mindset. My goal in sharing any of this advice with you has all been about helping you find fulfillment, purpose and happiness. The more any of us can find those things the better we'll all be, right?"

"Of course."

"Every night, when I'm lying in bed, I think of three things I'm grateful for. It can be people I interacted with during the day, outcomes from decisions I've made or even just having a roof over my head. It helps put me in a more peaceful, positive mindset. Even during the day, I try to keep that grateful attitude. I like how I feel and I truly think it affects how I interact and deal with other people."

"I guess I never really thought about it." Rory admitted.

"That's just it," C.J. said. "You have to be mindful of it. I know some people leave a note next to their bed as a reminder or write it down in a journal. I guarantee you that adopting a grateful mindset will change the way you view the world."

"That's a bold statement."

"It certainly is, but I believe it to my core." C.J. sat back in her chair with a big smile on her face. "I'm really proud of you Rory. You've done a great job in this process. I love that you've recognized that basketball is one of your true passions. Something that will bring you joy. Life is certainly about experiencing joy. You've also taken the effort to uncover all sorts of jobs in the industry; and that it's not just about being at the top. You've also made an effort to build your network of people who can possibly help you by learning from them and leveraging their connections. I'm sure they were all happy to help you because of your passion and enthusiasm. Maybe you'll be able to help them someday."

Rory smiled at the thought.

"Like we've discussed, these are the steps to gaining the experiences that lead to the right job fit and ultimately, fulfillment and happiness in your work because it's aligned with who you are. But don't forget, who you are can change along the way and that's okay. Be open to the idea that all your experiences make you grow as a person and you'll find new passions and interests. It's what makes life so rich. Hopefully we all keep experiencing, growing, learning and living."

"Can I get that on a t-shirt or a coffee mug?" Rory asked. They both laughed.

"All of this advice has been really, really helpful," Rory said. "I appreciate you challenging me to be introspective and think about what I truly am passionate about and giving me the confidence to not give up on that dream. I'm also grateful for all the advice you've given me on informational interviews, job shadows and internships. The experiences I've already gained talking with people have been so helpful. Your mentorship has been invaluable."

"Thanks for the kind words, Rory. I'm really glad we've been able to connect and that I've been able to help you along this journey. I know we talked about our next session together being our last."

Rory nodded.

"I was hoping you'd meet me downtown at one of my favorite places?"

"Absolutely!" Rory knew he'd follow C.J. anywhere.

"Great. Reilly will send you all the info. Looking forward to it, Rory."

"See you then!" Rory left C.J.'s office, intrigued about where she wanted to meet next.

Reilly was standing by her desk. "How did it go with C.J. today?"

"So good," Rory said. "She is the best."

"Yes she sure is. I've learned so much."

"Right, I bet. Working for her must be something else." For Rory, anything that drew out the conversation was great with him.

"I've heard horror stories from other personal assistants," Reilly said. "Not her. She is the real thing. A good person, through and through. With some very interesting ideas."

"Today it was meditation."

"Right! Learned that from her and now I love it," Reilly said.

"Meditation? You too?"

"Absolutely," Reilly said with that sparkle. "Don't knock it till you try it."

"Okay, you talked me into it," Rory said. "I'm just sorry that my sessions with C.J. are winding down soon."

"Oh really?"

Was that disappointment he glimpsed in Reilly's eyes?

"Winding down?"

"Yes, afraid so."

There was another silence.

"So... what are you doing this weekend, Rory?"

"Nothing. I mean, studying, working on my career stuff."
He stared down at his new shoes. He sensed an opportunity
passing him by. *Never quite good enough.*

"Uh, what about you?" he finally asked.

"Not much, same old."

"Ah, right."

Another pause.

"Well Rory, I hope wherever those fancy shoes take you, it's
great," Reilly said with a smile.

"You too," he said, knowing that didn't sound right, either.
He turned to go.

"Hey, I looked for you on social media," he said.
Immediately it sounded creepy to him.

"And?"

"You're a ghost. Not there."

"Ha! You're right. No Snapchat for me. No Insta-ham. No
taggin' and braggin'. I checked out of all that."

"Wow."

"Yep," Reilly said, looking him right in the eyes. "The only
me is right here."

It was his moment, and he blew it. He mumbled his
goodbyes and trudged away. As soon as he was outside, he
thought of about five ways he could have asked her out.

*Missed the chance. Missed the shot. Way out of your league
anyway. Guess you can't win at everything, there, Rory boy.*

Steps to Take

- Journal what you like and dislike about your job
  experiences. This will help you be more aware when making
  decisions on future opportunities.

- People grow and change. Give yourself space to like new things, even new industries, that might be more aligned with who you are. It's ok to modify and adjust your path based on your learnings.

- Cultivate a regular practice of exercise, meditation and gratitude. Taking care of your own mind and body is a key element to finding purpose, fulfillment and happiness.

twenty-three

The Puzzle Comes Together

As the next few weeks passed, Rory watched the DribbleSync website like a hawk, checking the Jobs section every day, sometimes more often. He was worse than a kid waiting for Christmas, he laughed to himself.

The moment he spotted the long-awaited product marketing internship posting, Rory pounced. Setting all else aside, he filled out the online application with care. One section in particular made him stop and think. That's where DribbleSync asked applicants to describe why they wanted the internship opportunity. Rory worked for a long time to be sure he said exactly what he wanted. Then he asked Xavier to read it and give him some feedback.

"Be gentle," Rory said. "I'm a little nervous to hear what you think, but I know I need your extra perspective. And a little proofing and editing help won't hurt either."

"At your service," Xavier said. "Here it is. I, Rory Langford, want this internship so I can get my friend and roommate Xavier a sweet new smart basketball. Excellent plan!"

Rory threw something at him. "Start over!"

"Okay." Xavier cleared his throat dramatically. "Why do I want this internship? Because I was meant to do this job. After graduating high school, I had no idea what to do in life. Then I met this amazing person and mentor, C.J., who has taught me so much. Step by step, she encouraged me to find my true purpose, to be more like me. I took each step seriously and put in the work. Little by little, a clear picture emerged. Today, I can tell you with confidence what I am here on this planet to do. I've talked to dozens of working professionals who've helped me shape that personal mission even more. I know what kind of people I want to work with, and what kind of company culture I want to be a part of. I know what I'm passionate about. I know what I'm good at. And where all those circles overlap? That is DribbleSync. Your company checks every single box. I'm in awe of everything I've learned about your company and what it stands for. If I could tell people I work for DribbleSync, I would do so with great pride. If it takes me 100 tries, I am determined to be a part of your team in some way. I'm willing to work harder and learn more than anyone you've seen, and I'm willing to do it all for free at this internship. That's how much I know I belong there."

Xavier took a deep breath. Then he applauded and shook Rory's hand.

"You, sir, are hired," he said.

"YES!" Rory said. "Thanks for the vote of confidence."

"It's really, really good," Xavier said. "If that doesn't get you the job, I don't know what will."

"Okay, then see what you think of this," Rory said. He showed Xavier a little product review video he'd made on his phone. Rory had borrowed a smart basketball for the day, and had a few of his buddies dribble it around, then tell him what they liked about the ball. He'd edited their remarks into a quick-moving clip with music and a few simple graphics. It had been a fun little project, and he'd done it all in a few hours.

"It's great," Xavier said. "Caught my attention the whole way, and that guy at the end cracks me up."

"Good deal," Rory said. "Exactly what I hoped for. I'm going to link to my promo video in my application. C.J. said it might help me stand out."

"Well good luck, my friend," Xavier said. "Looks to me like you've nailed it."

Later that afternoon, Rory was studying for his English 202 midterm at El Jefe's Coffee Shop.

"Hey Rory, how have you been?"

It was his friend Ally. They had been biology lab partners their freshman year.

"I've been well. Just getting some studying done and trying to line up an internship this summer."

"That's good," Ally said with a bright smile. She always seemed to be in a good mood. "Where at?"

"My first choice is DribbleSync. You heard of them?"

"The smart basketball?"

"Yep, exactly. But I'm doing some research on other companies and opportunities, hoping to increase my options."

"That's smart."

"What about you, Ally? I know you always talked about international business. Are you still thinking about that?"

"I'm still exploring it. I think it'd be interesting. I've got a lot to figure out. I did line up a neat opportunity though. It's a virtual internship."

"Oh yeah? I've never really heard of a virtual internship."

"I wanted to get some sort of job shadow or internship with an international company during the school year, but obviously, I still had to be here taking classes. So I did a bunch of research and found this company in London that does investments in startup companies all over the world. After looking on their website, I reached out to their human resources department and told them I wanted to do a virtual internship."

"Really? That's awesome."

"They were a little hesitant at first since they didn't understand what that meant. I explained that I wanted to work with someone on their finance team. I called it an internship mentor. I said I could help with small projects like building financial models, evaluating potential investment opportunities and creating presentations. It didn't have to be on actual deals they were working on. It could be mock projects just so I could get some experience. Then my internship mentor would give me feedback on the items I'd created via email and video chats."

"That's so smart," Rory said.

"They thought so too. They said it was an innovative idea and they were excited to work with me. They paired me with a woman who is the director of research. Our first video chat is next week, where we'll set some guidelines and talk about potential projects together. I'm super excited. Should be a great experience."

"Nicely done," Rory said. "That really is a great idea. I'd never thought of anything like that. The chance to do a virtual internship with a company anywhere in the world opens up a lot of possibilities. You don't have to limit yourself to local options. Very cool. Congratulations Ally."

"Thanks. I'll let you know how it goes."

"Can't wait to hear. Great to see you."

"You too, Rory. Take care."

The weeks flew by as he waited on pins and needles for news from DribbleSync. Finally the news arrived in his inbox. The subject line said, About Your Internship Application.

Drum roll please.

Breathe deep, it's only a job. It's okay either way.

Just click the thing. Let's read it.

So he did:

Rory,

We appreciate you applying for the product marketing internship position. Our team has thoroughly reviewed your application, along with many others who applied for the same position...

Go on. He drummed his fingers impatiently as he read.

At this time, we can inform you that...

The suspense!

...we have selected you as our next product marketing intern. Congratulations and welcome to DribbleSync.

Rory let out a victory scream that nearly tore the roof off his room. Anyone who heard it might have been tempted to call 911. "YES!"

He thought about everything that had led to this point. All the conversations with C.J. The late nights of research and introspection. The hard work. His first conversation with Jenny Chang from the Payton University basketball program who introduced him to Kari at DribbleSync. He wondered if his informational interview with her had helped him get the internship since she got to talk with him and hear more of his personality and interests.

He thought about his job shadow with the Elevate social media team and watching them make videos. He'd used some of their techniques they'd shared with him in his product review video for DribbleSync.

He'd learned a lot from each of those situations and they'd helped him make this internship a reality. He loved seeing the puzzle pieces come together.

His first call was to his mom. She shared a similar scream of joy on the other end of the line, and they rejoiced together.

His next call was to C.J., through Reilly's desk. Of course the reason was to thank C.J. for all the time she'd invested in him, and to find out how happy she'd be that it had paid off. Funny thing was, if the message got to Reilly first, that wouldn't hurt. For some reason he really wanted her to be proud of him, too.

The phone rang three times and Reilly's distinctively smooth and mirthful voice answered.

"You'll never guess what happened to me," Rory began.

Steps to Take

-   Think big when it comes to internships/apprenticeships. Even a virtual opportunity with a mentor or company halfway around the world can be a valuable experience. And maybe you're the one who will have to suggest it.

twenty-four

The Highest Tribute

Today was the day Rory would meet C.J. in some mysterious location. He'd gotten a call from Reilly just to be sure he'd be there.

"Rory?"

"Reilly!"

"Just a reminder," said that amazing voice. "You're meeting C.J. at 3 p.m. today, downtown on the corner of Third and Ash. Have fun."

He looked up the address on his phone. It sounded familiar, since he'd ridden the bus through that part of town before and had seen the small city park. When he arrived, C.J. was sitting alone on a bench. She waved hello and gestured for him to come sit down.

"Thanks for meeting me outside of the office this time," she said.

"Of course. I have to admit, I wasn't expecting to meet you in a city park. So this is one of your favorite places?"

She laughed.

"Well, not exactly this park bench. It's that building over there." She pointed to a nondescript brick building across the street. "That's the 3rd Avenue Youth Center. It's a place for under-resourced neighborhood kids to come after school."

"Under-resourced?"

"Yes, kids who, for a variety of reasons, just don't have all the benefits at home other kids do. It provides them a snack and some tutoring if they need it, but mostly it's a safe place to hang out and be a kid. This can be a tough neighborhood and a lot of these kids have a rough time of it. In an effort to help them thrive, we pair all the kids up with volunteer leaders who build relationships with them, listen to their stories and ultimately let them know they're valued."

"'We?"

"Yes, I'm on the board of directors of the Third Avenue Youth Center."

"You are? I should've guessed!"

"Rory, most of our time together has been focused on helping you identify what education, industries, connections and experiences can help you find a profession that aligns with your unique skills and interests. As you know, these things can bring greater fulfillment in your everyday work. Greater fulfillment is incredibly important to being happy. But I wanted to share with you a few other ways to find fulfillment, even purpose, that aren't necessarily tied to your work. It's the last phase of the IDEAS Framework: Service."

Rory sat up taller on the park bench, intrigued by what she was about to say.

"Everyone's sense of connection and obligation to the world around them comes at different times in their lives. Take a young child who doesn't understand why some people live on the streets and wonders what they can do about it, so they rally a blanket drive in an effort to help. Someone else, later in life, might feel a sense of gratitude toward the community they came from and want to do something to give back to make it a better place. Others recognize inequality around the world and step in to help offer the tools to a better life. And of course, there are so many other unique scenarios when it comes to being in the service of others."

"I remember a few times when Mom took me to the local homeless shelter to volunteer," Rory said. "I liked that feeling of doing something good. It also made me more grateful for the things we had in life."

"I believe we all feel that sense of connection to the world," C.J. said. "And to one another. For some, it's less intense than others, but nonetheless it's there. When we shed more light on it and really lean into it, we open ourselves to more opportunity for fulfillment and purpose. You really can't deny that charity work is a selfish act, because the giver can get so much out of it, but the beauty is, it also benefits the recipient. It's a win/win."

"I've seen it for myself," Rory said. "That sense of community you feel when you lend a hand. Whether it's an official volunteering effort or just helping someone because you see they need it. But how do you know where to start?"

"Great question. You've hit on another one of my burning interests," C.J. said. "Over the years, I've talked with a lot of different people about what excites and motivates them when it comes to donating their time or money. I've found those reasons, and causes, are as varied as people themselves. There are charities, movements and causes of all kinds. Maybe it's helping children or underserved communities. Maybe you're passionate about education, helping the elderly or lending aid to people in a third-world country. There are endless opportunities to get involved."

"Interesting," Rory said. "In a way, it sounds like the same process for finding your job fit. Start by being introspective and understanding what excites and motivates you and then getting out and trying a few things. You could even apply the IDEAS Framework if you wanted."

"Wow! Maybe you really have been listening this whole time, after all," C.J. said.

They laughed together.

"You're so right," she said. "When you get aligned with something that really moves you and you're passionate about it, then you'll usually do more good and stick to it longer. But like a job fit, you also have to recognize that we grow and change as humans. Your interests might stay with the same cause for years, or you might find you want to get involved with other things. And that's okay."

"What inspired you? I've heard my Mom talk about some of your charitable work. How did you first get involved?"

"It's certainly been a journey. My connection to giving back started pretty young when my parents took us to the Giving Tree around Christmas time. You've probably heard of something like it. An organization finds out the needs of under-resourced families, like clothes, books and toys, and puts tags up on a Christmas tree for others to come and anonymously buy for those families. My parents made it fun, and turned it into a family outing where we went shopping in order to benefit someone else. It's my earliest memory of starting to understand the needs of others outside of myself. The realization that with a simple act you could bring some happiness and comfort to someone else. As I got older, I did a little volunteer work here and there and even took my own children to a local Giving Tree. I wanted to pass on that same feeling I had when I was their age. Then I was asked to join the board of directors here at the Third Avenue Youth Center. As a board member, our job is to make sure the organization is running smoothly and carrying out the mission to help these kids. I also started donating money to the organization because

I wanted to further the good work they were doing. It felt great to be a part of it and helping those neighborhoods."

Rory could see the fire in C.J.'s eyes.

"I found over time that I was also passionate about education. Whether that was volunteering my time to speak in classrooms, inspiring kids to think about new career opportunities or helping start new schools in my community. I've come to understand how my unique skills and interests can benefit others in this world and I tried to use them the best way I knew how. So now my charitable work is a mix between volunteering my time by sitting on several boards of organizations I care about, helping out at a food bank or homeless shelter when I can, speaking to students like you whenever possible and also donating money to the causes I really care about. A lot of people think charity is just donating money, but donating your own time can be so much more rewarding and valuable and doesn't cost you anything. An easy way to get started is Googling volunteer opportunities in your own town."

"It's pretty great to see how passionate you are about giving back. Why do you think that is?" Rory wanted to dig a little deeper, but he didn't want to get too personal.

"You've heard of the golden rule?"

"Treating others the way you want to be treated?"

"Exactly. I guess for me, it really comes down to that. Feeling that connection to others and wondering how I can help. If I was in their situation, I hope someone would have the compassion and desire to help me. We're all humans. Maybe we're in different places in our lives, financially, emotionally and geographically, but we're still connected by our humanity and it's important we fight for equity. Thurgood Marshall, the first African-American Supreme Court Justice once said, *In recognizing the humanity of our fellow beings, we pay ourselves the highest tribute.*"

Rory let that sink in for a minute.

"It's so true," he said. "Even with our many differences, we're all on this earth together, all striving to live our lives and to be our best. We have to take care of one another."

"You know, there's another way to blend your professional life with your passion for helping others," C.J. said.

"Yes?"

"You can decide to go to work for those non-profit organizations or benefit corporations that are helping do good in the world. It's a great way to make a difference, make a living and bring purpose to your work."

"It reminds of my friend Laura," Rory said. "For as long as I've known her, she's talked about starting a non-profit organization in Africa, helping people become more self-sufficient in remote villages."

"Good for Laura," C.J. said. "You should help continue to encourage her in the direction of that dream. Whether you integrate volunteering into your life or make it your job, this is a great way to find purpose and fulfillment, which can ultimately foster more happiness. We all want to be more fulfilled in our lives. And trust me, simply making more money doesn't automatically lead to happiness like most people want to believe."

"I could see myself volunteering at an after-school program in a gym."

"Wait, you? Basketball?"

They enjoyed a moment of shared laughter.

"Well, come on," C.J. said. "I want to take you inside so you can see the place in action. And introduce you to Fayda, our executive director. She's amazing."

"Absolutely," Rory said. "Let's do it."

Inside, throughout the tour, he found himself very impressed by the center, the kids and the staff. He recognized that warm feeling that came from doing something important for others. He'd felt great being in the youth center and he wasn't even the one volunteering. He was determined to find a cause that he could learn more about and start to invest some of his time. C.J had shown him firsthand the importance of finding time to give back. Once again, he owed her so much. He hoped he would be worthy of her time and effort. Maybe someday, he could even repay the favor.

/ twenty-five /

A Chat With the Boss

"Rory, could I see you in my office?"

"Absolutely, Kari. I'll be right there."

Rory smiled. He realized that question might prompt fear at some jobs. But not here at DribbleSync. Over the course of his all-too-short summer internship, he'd come to anticipate these regular one-on-one conversations Kari liked to have with her employees. She called them her check-in chats.

"Have a seat, Rory," she said. "Well, your last day on the job. I'm going to miss our chats."

"Yes, I am too," Rory said.

"I have to tell you, I'm really impressed with what you've done here in your short time with us at DribbleSync."

"That feels amazing to hear."

"I'm serious. You've really made a name for yourself. What are your plans from here?"

"Back to school this fall, and believe it or not I'm really enjoying my industrial engineering classes. I've also decided to get a concentration in marketing. I've set a goal to do at least five informational meetings with a mix of some local companies and some across the country. I also want to do at least two job shadows of different roles in marketing and manufacturing. I plan to use the Payton University career resources and attend their career fairs."

"That's an ambitious list that will pay off," Kari said.

"It's really been fun working here, Kari. I've enjoyed getting to know you and the other members of your team. I have to tell you, I appreciate your management style."

"Thanks for saying so, Rory. What do you like in particular?"

"Well, I like these chats. And I like the fact that you've welcomed me to ask questions any time I need to. Not all bosses are like that."

"No, they're not," Kari said. "In fact, I've worked for people who kept their door shut and sort of ruled by intimidation. I think that's what made me take another route as a boss."

"It works," Rory said. "I see the positive ripple effect through your team."

"Any other feedback for me?"

"Yes, thanks for asking. I also appreciate the way you've always given clear direction on what you expected, but allowed me the space to get it done. I like the way I've been encouraged to collaborate with other interns from the product marketing department and others across the company. There's definitely a sense of teamwork and camaraderie."

"Glad you noticed, Rory. That's very important to me."

"I felt like DribbleSync was good at appreciating the hard work and contributions that everyone's making. That time you gave me a shout out at the all-company meeting for the work we did on the social media research project? That felt great."

"Well-deserved for sure."

"But not all bosses would do that. And I'm grateful for the way you encouraged me to make friends with people in the manufacturing, finance and sales departments and connect with them on LinkedIn. Like C.J. always told me, You never know who might be able to help you in the future. Maybe I can even help them someday."

"I have no doubt, Rory. In my mind you've got big things ahead of you."

"Well, no small part of that is thanks to you," Rory said. "And now, could I ask you for some feedback in turn?"

"Go right ahead."

"With my internship coming to a close here, I'd like some feedback on my performance. I want to know not only what I did well, but also what I need to work on. I want to grow professionally, and I want to always be in a growth mindset, to learn and get better."

"Good mindset! We can always use more of that around here," Kari said. She paused and pursed her lips.

"Hmm. Let's see. I appreciate the way you always show up early and prepared. I appreciate your positive approach. And I appreciate the way you made a point of getting along with everyone around you. You're at ease around people and you build them up. Those qualities are a big deal."

"Then I'll keep it up," Rory said.

"As far as things to work on? Basically the same advice I always give myself. Always be in process improvement mode. Try to challenge yourself each day to do better than the day before. Find your weaknesses and spend the most time on those things. If you find it hard to talk in front of people, do more public speaking. If you find yourself weak in some area, personally or professionally, spend more time there. And here's another thing I've found helpful. Don't act like you're just an intern, or front line employee. Whenever you do a job, work as if you are already at the next level. Dress the part and conduct yourself like a leader. That will help you rise above the menial concerns of every day, and work on the longer game. That goes for conduct, conversation, and focus."

When she said that, Kari looked right at him. She didn't talk about specifics, but Rory thought back to a few times over the summer where he'd been part of some petty, unproductive conversations with other employees, and a handful of meetings where he showed up unprepared. Not leadership behavior.

"Thank you for all of that. I will take your advice," he said.

Then Rory took a deep breath and asked the question that had been on his mind all summer. In the past, he would have been too intimidated to ask directly. But the new Rory, with his clear personal and professional goals, along with his daily meditation and exercise habits, was a new person entirely.

"I'd like to work here when I graduate from school," he said. "What do I need to do?"

Kari's eyebrows lifted.

"That's a compliment to our company," she said. "And I'm happy to hear you say it. At the same time, you and I both know there will be a lot of water under the bridge before then. So let's leave it like this. You are exactly the kind of candidate I'd like to hire here full time at DribbleSync. If you keep working on those things we talked about, you'll be even more qualified. Please stay in touch, and I would be happy to have you walk into my office the day you graduate."

Rory stood and shook her hand.

"Kari, you're a great boss and I would be proud to work for you again," he said.

Walking back to his little office nook for the last time, he was already more conscious of how he conducted himself. When someone called out, "Hey Rory, you playing hoops this weekend?" he didn't stop to talk. He smiled, nodded and said, "You bet. I'll see you there."

As he packed up his few personal belongings, his phone rang. Normally he didn't take personal calls at work, but he recognized the number. He grabbed his backpack and stepped out into the hallway.

"Hello?"

"Rory, this is Emma."

Curiously, his heart didn't do its old backflips at the sound of her voice.

"Emma, this is quite a surprise. Haven't heard anything from you in a long time."

"Yes, sorry I've been out of touch, but I wanted to change all that."

"You do?"

"Yes, I ran into someone from Payton who told me what you've been up to. Sounds like you're a winner these days, Rory."

"Every day is a new chance. I'm doing my best."

"That doesn't sound like the you I remember."

"And what are you doing now, Emma? How are you?"

"Well, school wasn't working, and I couldn't figure out what to do next. So I took whatever job I could find. I'm at a coffee stand. I'm not really sure what I want to do with the rest of my life."

"I know what that feels like.""

"So, since it's Friday night, me and some friends are going out, and wondered if you wanted to go with me."

"Sounds like you'll have fun," Rory said.

"It can be just like old times again, Rory."

"Emma, I appreciate that you called, but I can't go out with you tonight, or any night."

"You can't? Why not?"

"I have a dinner date," he said.

"A date?"

"Take good care of yourself, Emma."

He ended the call and paused a moment.

And then a voice rang out behind him in the hallway, a playful voice as rich as honey.

"How about it, Mr. Langford? Ready to take me to dinner?"

He turned.

In that moment, Reilly was the most beautiful thing he had ever seen.

/ twenty-six /

A Grateful State of Mind

It was the end of another long day for Rory Langford, proud college graduate and product marketing specialist. A long day but a good one. There was a big deadline and he'd decided to arrive at 6 a.m. today. That meant getting up at 4:30 a.m. to get in his exercise and meditation. Now it was late afternoon and he was still hard at the job.

But he had discovered something fascinating. At times like these, hours passed without effort. Time flew by before he could even look up from his work. He found himself totally absorbed in the task at hand. His company was leading their industry and he was excited and proud to play his part.

He had kept to his plan and graduated Payton in industrial engineering with a marketing minor. He'd explored a number of opportunities in the basketball industry, but all roads kept leading back to DribbleSync. Kari had been delighted to offer him the job, and the team had welcomed him back with open arms.

In the year he'd worked here at DribbleSync, he'd been able to work on some really great campaigns for the newest release, the DS5. He was the product specialist assigned to the social media team. He attended events, met famous athletes and even worked the DribbleSync booth at the NCAA Final Four weekend. That was an amazing experience.

The job was not without its challenges. Often, like today, the days were long. There were times when the work was tedious. Sometimes he wondered what it would be like to work at another company instead. During these times, his mom reminded him how lucky he was to be in an industry he loved. C.J. assured him those feelings were normal, and that not every day was exciting as the first day on the job. Kari was supportive as a boss. And Reilly, sweet Reilly, never failed to praise his victories and soothe him in any defeats.

He had an amazing job, and he was excelling at it. These days those weary feelings were few and far between, but when they came, the act of centering himself always brought him back to a grateful state of mind. *Wow,* he would think. *I have a job in basketball.*

He kept a daily journal of what he liked and what he didn't about his work. C.J. had given him this idea too, a way to be more introspective and adaptable for future opportunities. She said it was all about learning in an effort to be more aligned with his authentic self. This was the path to fulfillment, purpose and happiness. Thanks to her influence, he had even reached out to a local non-profit organization to see about volunteering. There wasn't a day that went by that he wasn't grateful for something C.J. had taught him. In fact, in the middle of his very busy day today, he'd asked Reilly to help him arrange a special delivery to C.J.'s office.

First to arrive, last one to leave.

He'd always heard those stories about Michael Jordan's work ethic. Today, Rory was putting in those kinds of hours himself. He shut down his computer and rubbed his neck. He was the only one left in the office. As he turned off the lights for the evening, his phone rang.

"Hi, is this Mr. Langford?" said a voice asked on the other end.

"Yes, it is."

"I'm glad I found you. My name is Marie St. Claire. I'm a freshman at Payton University. I saw through our alumni network that you are working at DribbleSync. Is that right?"

Rory grinned to himself, there in the darkened office.

"Yes, I do work here at DribbleSync in product marketing. What can I do for you, Marie?"

"Well, I'm still trying to figure out what I want to do with my life, but I'm really interested in learning more about jobs in product marketing. I was wondering if you'd be willing to schedule an informational interview with me in the near future?"

The smile widened across Rory's face. "Marie, I would absolutely love to."

He walked out of the office humming happily to himself.

He pondered a moment, then dug his phone out of his pocket again and called what was by now a familiar number.

"Yes Rory?"

"C.J., I wonder if you have any idea how a certain Marie St. Claire thought to track me down for an interview," he said.

There was silence on the other end of the line, then a chuckle.

"Well, you've caught me," she said. "Marie is my newest protege. She wanted the best and I told her to find you. But I'll only admit to that if you can explain how this beautiful vase of tulips ended up on my desk today. The guilty party even somehow knew my favorite kind of flower. And the thank-you note, although strangely anonymous, might have been written by Shakespeare himself."

It was Rory's turn to laugh.

"C.J., I could send you a new thank you every day and never express my appreciation enough. Thanks to the IDEAS Framework steps you took me through, I'm really and truly living my dream. I have more confidence, I'm in better shape and I'm happier than I've ever been."

"Not to mention the romance that's blossomed," she teased him.

"You've changed my life," Rory said.

"You did the work yourself, Rory. I just helped point you in the right direction."

"How will I ever thank you?"

"You can start by helping Marie. She's really jumping from one thing another right now. She needs some sound advice."

"Well, a very wise person once told me there is no such thing as losing, just learning," Rory said with a smile. "And there is a wonderful method that always works to find your purpose, that is if you're willing to put in the work. It all starts with Introspection… And it ends with a way to *Be More Like You*."

twenty-seven

A Shot to Remember

It was the first day of the Blue Devils junior basketball clinic.

"Today," said Coach, "we are proud to welcome back Rory Langford."

The Blue Devils let out a cheer as Rory walked onto the court. He took a deep breath of the same familiar Pine-Sol and sweat. The memories flooded back.

"We're lucky to have Mr. Langford today," Coach said. "He was a star point guard here, and he's worked his way up to head of marketing at DribbleSync. He's going to show us how their newest smart basketball works. And maybe give us some pointers on improving our game. Mr. Langford volunteers his time at youth camps and clinics all over the state."

The players applauded as Rory stepped forward.

"Show us how your new ball works," Coach said.

Rory looked at the young faces in a circle, watching his every move. He felt the weight of the ball in his hands. But he was ready. He'd practiced this play a million times.

Langford takes the pass, the defender guarding him tight. Langford fakes the drive. He steps back, creates space, he gets off the shot...

Once again, Rory jumped and released. Once again, the ball arced through space as if forever.

But this time, there was nothing but net.

Acknowledgements

I am so thankful for the many people who have always had my back and believed I had a few ideas worth sharing:

God - Thank you for leading the way.

Kelly, Allie, Lauren and Ryan - Just want to say thanks again. I love you.

Mom - My biggest fan. Thanks for always being the loudest cheerleader. Your belief in me always carried me on when I didn't always believe in myself.

Dad - Thanks for becoming my best friend and holding me to the highest standards (because you always believed I could achieve them).

Hollidays/Johnsens/Farringtons/Orts - There is no better family support team than you.

Nick Murto/Jeff Oswalt/Ramsey Pruchnic - I'm grateful for our partnerships. You've allowed me to do things I never could have on my own. Appreciate your support and inspiration.

The employees at Seven2, 14Four, Strategy Labs, The Union Studios and Method Juice Cafe - Your commitment to great work always leaves me in awe. Thank you.

Chad Dashiell / Ryan Miller / Matt Kinder / Tom Davis - You always shoot it to me straight and don't let me use excuses. I'm grateful for your accountability and friendship.

Shane Atchison - You kindly got me an internship (Accelerated Media) so many years ago that sparked my love for digital marketing. You've mentored and inspired me ever since. I don't think you'll ever know the depth of my gratitude.

Andre Lewis - You're a true friend. Thank you for navigating the seas of service with me.

Shelly O'Quinn - Thank you for always encouraging me to step into my passion for education. I always learn something new watching you lead.

Claire Manley - I have been so lucky to have you on the team. Your encouragement, critical insights and commitment to excellence have made these pages even richer. Someday, I'll be working for you.

David Kilmer - You truly wield a fanciful magic for aligning the right words in the right way to convey just the right message. Your influence as an editor was felt far and wide throughout these pages.

Kristin Goff - Little do you know, your kind and wonderful words of encouragement regarding this subject were a catalyst for putting it into a book.

Father Greg Boyle - Your book, *Tattoos on the Heart*, will forever be the NorthStar for how I strive to see humanity.

Jesse Pierpoint / Jon Deviny / Ariel Lewis / Eric Smith / Callen Fulbright / Hugh Russell / Krista Yep / Joe Haeger / Mike Miller - I am so incredibly grateful for your creative contributions to this project. I am lucky I get to stand on your shoulders.

Notes

Vallerand, Robert. "On the Psychology of Passion: In Search of What Makes People's Lives Most Worth Living." *Presidential address given at the 68th Canadian Psychological Association Annual Convention, in Ottawa, Ontario,* June 2007.

Oliver, Laura. "Ikigai: Is this Japanese concept the secret to a long, happy, meaningful life?" *World Economic Forum*, August 2007.

Epstein, David. "Range: Why Generalists Triumph in a Specialized World." *Riverhead Books,* May 2019.

Dweck, Carol. "Mindset: The New Psychology of Success." *Ballantine Books,* December 2007.

Abdul-Jabbar, Kareem. "Great players are willing to give up their own personal achievement for the achievement of the group. It enhances everybody." *Becoming Kareem: Growing Up On and Off the Court,* November 2017.

16 Personalities 16personalities.com/free-personality-test

Myers Briggs Type Indicator mbtionline.com

Enneagram truity.com/test/enneagram-personality-test

Clifton Strengths gallup.com/cliftonstrengths

LinkedIn linkedin.com

About the Author

Tyler is a serial entrepreneur with businesses in the digital advertising, media, health and fitness industries. For more than twenty years, he's also been following his own passion of helping students dream big and discover new career opportunities through mentorship, speaking in classrooms and developing and online platform connecting professionals and educators called Access2Experience. He's an active member of his community through leadership and philanthropy and lives with his family in the Pacific Northwest.

Printed in Great Britain
by Amazon

87665508R00112